D0269067

WAY *of*
Hinduism

Stephen Cross

WOLVERHAMPTON LIBRARIES			
ALL			9 SEP 2002
0007 136110 8829 19			
294. 5 CRO			
F			C685946

0007 136110 8829 19

Thorsons
An Imprint of HarperCollins*Publishers*
77–85 Fulham Palace Road
Hammersmith, London W6 8JB

The Thorsons website address is:
www.thorsons.com

and *Thorsons*
are trademarks of HarperCollins*Publishers* Limited

First published by Element Books Ltd as
The Elements of Hinduism 1994
This edition published by Thorsons 2002

1 3 5 7 9 10 8 6 4 2

© Stephen Cross 1994

Stephen Cross asserts the moral right to be
identified as the author of this work

A catalogue record for this book
is available from the British Library

ISBN 0 00 713611 0

Printed and bound in Great Britain by
Martins the Printers Limited, Berwick upon Tweed

All rights reserved. No part of this publication may be
reproduced, stored in a retrieval system, or transmitted,
in any form or by any means, electronic, mechanical,
photocopying, recording or otherwise, without the prior
written permission of the publishers.

Contents

Notes and Further Material

Stephen Cross has been closely involved with Hindu thought for many years and is a frequent visitor to India. Before turning to writing he was a documentary film producer based in London, making films for television on the culture and religion of peoples in many parts of the world. Subsequently he studied Sanskrit and Indian thought at the University of Sydney. He is a Fellow of the Royal Asiatic Society, frequently lectures on subjects to do with India in Sydney and London, and has contributed articles to journals in Australia, Britain and the USA. He currently lives in Sydney.

Acknowledgements

Grateful thanks are due to the President of the Shri Ramakrishna Math, Mylapore, Madras, for permission to reproduce the drawings of Hindu deities.

The author wishes to thank Dr A J Alston of London, and Dr Michael Comans, formerly of the Centre for Indian Studies, University of Sydney, for reading the draft and making a number of valuable suggestions. The late Ruth Komon, of the Australian School of Yoga, Sydney, kindly gave her expert advice on the sections concerning the Yoga tradition.

The knowledge that this spirit, which is essentially one, is in one's own and in all other bodies, is the great end, or true wisdom, of one who knows the unity and the true principles of things. As one diffusive air, passing through the perforations of a flute, is distinguished as the notes of the scale, so the nature of the great spirit is single, though its forms be manifold.

Vishnu Purana

Introduction

It is no secret that we in the West live in a time of spiritual crisis. For almost two thousand years Europe has been guided by the insights of Christianity, and Western civilization has reflected this in many ways. Now, to many, that period appears to be drawing to a close, and the religious and social structures associated with it are in disarray. The old certainties deriving from the Christian world-view have gone, and modern man finds himself with little to guide him.

There is a positive side to this process. As the old, closed world has cracked asunder, Western man has come into contact with other religions and different world-views. Of these, some, like Islam, derive from the same Semitic tradition as Christianity, and share many features with it. Others – Hinduism, Buddhism, Taoism – are from regions much further removed from our own, both physically and intellectually; they offer radically different perspectives and demand a correspondingly greater change in our understanding. What have long been basic assumptions of Western thought – the reality of the external world, the soul as a simple substance, the linear nature of time – are called into question. Bridges are needed to these different worlds of thought and of spiritual experience, and it is in an effort to provide one such bridge that the present book is written.

In the case of Hinduism, once the crossing has been made many find that what lies on the other side, and behind the lush tangle of religious imagery, is a surprisingly clear structure of thought. Hindus have always been metaphysicians at heart. For them it is the underlying ideas, and not the imagery in which they are clothed, which ultimately count. It is these ideas, rather than the gods and myths which express them, which will be given most attention in this book.

The word Hindu was originally a geographical rather than a religious term. It was first used in the Persian Empire, and then by the Greeks who followed Alexander in his conquests, for those who lived around the banks of the great Indus river system in what is today the Punjab. The Indians we call Hindus do not among themselves use that term for their religion. To them it is *vaidika-dharma*, the Vedic religion, or simply *sanatana-dharma*, the eternal religion, the primordial tradition as it has been since the first unrolling of the universe. If asked his religion, such a man is likely to answer that he is a worshipper of this or that deity – of Vishnu or Rama, Krishna or Shiva or Durga. Thus an illusion of polytheism arises. That he is a Hindu is simply taken for granted, for to those born within its fold it seems so normal, natural and timeless as hardly to need a name.

We in the West often think of Hinduism as ancient and unchanging. Ancient it certainly is, but the forms of Hinduism are not, and have rarely ever been, static. On the contrary, they have exhibited an almost continuous development. What *is* unchanging is the bedrock of metaphysical principles upon which Hinduism rests, and this is symbolized by the special position accorded to the Vedas, the sacred texts regarded as unalterable truth. But the forms in which, for the purposes of worship, these truths are clothed are many and changing: 'The once all-important and all-powerful Indra was demoted to the rank of a minor deity ruling over one of the quarters. His lieutenant Vishnu was elevated to the central place in the Trinity. Rudra, the terrible, became Shiva the auspicious. Many other deities like Dyaus, Aryaman and Pushan were quietly despatched into oblivion!'[1]

In the early Vedic period we hear only of those gods who entered India with the first Aryan settlers – Indra, Mitra, Varuna and the rest. Little by little other gods crept, fought or danced their way into the Hindu pantheon, among them the two great incarnations of Vishnu,

Rama and Krishna; the elephant-headed god, Ganesha; and the Mother Goddess, Mahadevi, in her various guises as Parvati or Uma, Durga or Kali. Some of these, it is thought, were the ancient gods of the land, older even than the Aryan invasions.

One of the ways in which Hinduism differs strikingly from those religions which we in the West are most used to is that it has no fixed minimum of doctrine. There is no Hindu creed and no central authority, no Vatican or Pope. Hinduism is not a tightly defined religion but rather the way of thought of an entire ancient and populous civilization. In the words of a distinguished Indian writer: 'Almost bewildering is the variety of doctrines that go under the name of Hinduism. It is customary to regard every man of religion as a believer in a personal Deity. But so far as Hinduism is concerned, this is not an essential requirement. One may be a Hindu and yet not believe that the ultimate reality is a God endowed with the attributes of personality. Even those Hindus who consider the plenary being to be a personal God conceive of Him in different ways.'[2]

Naturally this makes it difficult to define Hinduism, yet this is characteristic, for Indian thought mistrusts too great a use of exclusive definitions. Whereas in the West the tendency is to analyse, define and differentiate, in Hinduism it is to synthesize, and the emphasis is on continuity and common ground. It is not of course that Hinduism is without form. It has – as even a cursory glance will confirm – a plethora of forms, but these tend to be fluid and to pass easily into one another. For this reason the government of India, when seeking a legal definition of the term Hindu, found it could do no better than to define a Hindu as a person who is generally acknowledged as a Hindu by those among whom he lives!

Another and widely used way of defining a Hindu is as a person who accepts the authority of the Vedas in religious matters. Thus the Buddha and his followers, who reject Vedic authority, are not generally regarded as Hindus. Neither are the Sikhs, whose religion centres on their own holy book and gurus. Yet in the end even this definition will not quite do. Many Hindus have come to regard the Buddha as the tenth incarnation of Vishnu, while others insist that the idea that Buddhism is radically distinct from Hinduism is a Western misinterpretation. What is perhaps the greatest annual festival in all of India, that of Lord Jagganath (a form of Krishna) at Puri in Orissa, is thought by scholars to be in origin a Buddhist festival – the district of Puri was for long the home of one of the most sacred relics of the Buddhist world. So we see that the borders defining Hinduism remain fluid.

Nevertheless, the Vedas, often spoken of as *shruti*, are central for Hinduism. The four original books, together with the accretions which have gathered round them, play a role which is comparable to that of revelation in Semitic religions. Much of their tremendous prestige derives from what is undoubtedly a very great antiquity. The oldest parts of the Vedas contain the religious poetry of the Aryan people, who entered India sometime during the second millennium B.C. and left an indelible mark upon its culture. This early Vedic religion, centred upon sacrifices to the gods, is still conserved as an element within Hinduism by India's priestly class, the Brahmins.

The second source of the prestige of the Vedas lies in the last element to be included within them, the Upanishads. Most of these belong to the period between the ninth and the third centuries B.C. They record the teachings of the forest-dwelling *rishis* – saints, seers and sages who had attained or were close to *moksha* or *mukti*, 'release', the highest end of life. Their insights, essentially mystical in character, are central for later Hinduism, and for important sections constitute its ultimate authority.

In the language of myth, the Vedas are eternal; they are of divine, not human, origin and infallible in their own sphere. What is meant by this is that they record eternal spiritual laws and come to us from a source superior to that of the empirical and rational knowledge to which we are normally confined. This source is the intuitive and direct insights of the ancient *rishis*, which have been verified by sages in every subsequent generation. Knowledge based upon the senses, and reasoning based upon that, can tell us nothing about spiritual reality which belongs to a completely different order of being. Should the reports of those liberated in life be false then all is lost, for we have nothing else to go on. The Vedas are an authority in spiritual matters because in this sphere they are our only source of knowledge. But it does not follow that the Vedas are infallible in all areas. In other areas of life, those open to sense perception and the other valid means of knowledge recognized by Hindu thought, the Vedas are *not* an authority. Shankara, perhaps the greatest of Hindu philosophers, writes:

> A hundred shrutis *may declare, that fire is cold or*
> *that it is dark; still, they posses no authority in*
> *the matter ... we should in no way attach to*
> shruti *a meaning which is opposed to other*
> *authorities.*[3]

Because of this clear distinction Hinduism has not come into conflict with scientific views in the manner of some other religions.

WAY of

Two great traditions, both originating in the Vedas, run throughout the course of Hinduism, giving rise to different forms. The tension between them gives to Hinduism much of its character. They depend on different views of the ultimate reality, or Brahman as it is called in the Upanishads.

One tradition is theistic. It thinks of Brahman as a Personal God (usually Vishnu or Shiva), and does not differ essentially from the Western idea of God: Brahman has qualities by which we can know Him. He is all-powerful. He is benevolent. He responds to human love. He creates the universe, sustains and protects it, and will one day withdraw it into His own being from which it will once again come forth.

The other tradition is more uniquely Indian. Reality in its ultimate nature is beyond all forms and consequently beyond the reach of the mind. If it is truly *ultimate* reality it can have no parts or internal divisions, and hence no qualities; nor can there be any other principle which stands over against it. Reality can only be one. For this tradition the concept of a Personal God – a Brahman with qualities – is valid at its own level, but it is not the highest Brahman, not the ultimate truth. That lies beyond the differentiations on which the idea of a Personal God depends. The highest Brahman is *A-dvaita*, that is to say, 'Non Dual'. For this tradition, Brahman is conceived impersonally, or rather as supra-personal. Brahman is pure awareness, pure consciousness; or, as is sometimes said, *sat-cit-ananda*, 'being-consciousness-bliss' conceived as a single undifferentiated reality. Both traditions find support in the Upanishads, which sometimes speak of Brahman in personal terms using the masculine pronoun, and at other times in impersonal terms using the neuter pronoun.[4]

Although the over-arching reality which the Upanishads call Brahman is in itself one and single, from the human standpoint it is the underlying reality of all that is and therefore appears under an infinity of aspects. These different aspects of the one reality are symbolized by the many gods and goddesses of Hinduism. For example, Brahma (not to be confused with the over-arching Brahman) is that reality in its role as creator of the universe; in Vishnu it is seen as the preserver and upholder of the universe; and Shiva is that same reality viewed as the principle of transcendence which will one day 'destroy' the universe. These are the Trimurti, the 'three forms', and they are not so much different gods as different ways of looking at the same God. Each emphasizes a particular aspect or function of the one reality, and because of this each can be seen – and is seen by those specially devoted to him – as representing that reality itself. The forms are many, the reality is one; the principle is very deeply rooted in Hindu thought, and was stated at the very outset in the Rig Veda:

> *They call him Indra, Mitra, Varuna, Agni,*
> *And he is heavenly nobly-winged Garutman.*
> *To what is One, sages give many a title:*
> *They call it Agni, Yama, Matarisvan.*[5]

It is the same with all the gods and goddesses: they are not rivals but aspects of a single principle. The Hindu devotee, while he will generally have one particular form of god – his or her *ishta deva*, or chosen deity – on whom his devotion centres, moves easily between one god and another. A devotee of Shiva will, as a rule, readily worship Vishnu if the occasion arises – seeing in him only another, somewhat less central, expression of the same underlying reality.

The same idea carries over into the human sphere. Krishna and Rama are not strictly speaking gods, but *avataras*, 'descents' – human incarnations of Vishnu – for since he is the 'upholder' of the world it is he who descends in this way to protect it. In the same way, one's own Guru, or spiritual guide, can be seen as an incarnation of God – for ideally a Guru is one who has identified completely with his own innermost reality, and that reality is, in all that lives, divinity itself. It is not the Guru as an individual human being who is worshipped and served, but the Guru as Brahman, as supreme reality.

From what has been said it might be supposed that religious forms are unimportant to Hindus. This is far from being the case. All over India they are loved and worshipped and taken with great seriousness. No one who has watched Indians passionately celebrating the birthday of Lord Krishna could suppose that Hindus are indifferent to religious forms. And yet it remains true that behind this worship, and even among men and women of very simple background, the consciousness that the form they are worshipping represents a supra-formal principle, and that this is its true reality, is rarely altogether absent. It is not the form, but the god who is thought of as having descended into it, which is under worship. Anyone who has seen Indian villagers worshipping, let us say, the lovingly decorated image of Durga on her festival day, and then, at the end of the ceremonies, placing that same image into a pond or river where it rapidly dissolves, knows that this is so. The forms of religion, indispensable as these are, are not the same thing as the truths they represent.

One important effect of this is found in the tolerance which is widely admitted to mark the Hindu outlook. Like other religions Hinduism is divided into many sects and movements, and no one would claim that religious rivalries are unknown. Yet the worst traps of dogmatism are generally avoided. Personal choice in religion is universally respected; religious wars among Hindus are virtually unknown to history. And the understanding of the provisional nature of religious forms extends to other creeds. Hindus see these as alternative paths leading to the same mountain summit, and so as a rule they do not feel the need to proselytize. To the eager followers of other faiths this may appear as a mark of weakness or indifference, but this is to misunderstand. It is the logical outcome of Hindu metaphysics: *all* forms are provisional and ultimately unreal, and this applies to the forms of religion as to everything else. Even the Vedas themselves become valueless on the attainment of *moksha* or liberation – of no more value than is a well in a land which is flooded, as the Bhagavad Gita puts it.[6]

Moreover, the truth can only be one, so that those who approach it – and all peoples do to some extent – must necessarily speak in broadly similar terms, though the colouring derived from differing cultures will vary. It is only the failure to identify clearly the core of meaning in each of the great religions, and to disentangle it from the cultural accretions and mythological imagery which often gather so thickly round it – and, let us remember, which give it vivid life and power – which gives the misleading appearance of a fundamental divergence. In Europe, where it has sometimes gone under the name of the Perennial Philosophy, this vision of the underlying unity of religion has never been entirely lost sight of, but it is perhaps an especial glory of Hinduism that nowhere has it been more clearly and consistently seen than in India. So, far from shutting us within the closed framework of a system, Hinduism, by constantly recalling that our minds are themselves a part of the world-illusion, forces us to keep ourselves open to what lies beyond the mind and the world in which it lives.

WAY of

Finally, Hinduism differs from the religions with which we are more familiar in having no historic founder – no Jesus, or Muhammad, or Buddha – and no fixed point in time at which it can be said to begin. Hinduism, it is said, is like the Ganges, the great river which it holds especially sacred and celebrates as a goddess. Like the Ganges, it offers its benefits to all; children may splash and play in its shallows, and yet the boldest and most experienced swimmers cannot plumb its depths. Having her origin high among the snows of the Himalayan peaks – mountains have always symbolized high spiritual states – Ganga descends to the world of man and of everyday life, bringing her great flood of life-giving waters to the hot and dusty plains of northern India. As she progresses, tributaries, great and small streams which also have their beginnings high among the mountains, flow into her, swelling her volume and joining her in her progress to her ultimate home, the infinitude of the ocean.

So it is with Hinduism. Although we can trace its course very far – it is the oldest of the great religions – its ultimate origins lie beyond even the early Vedic period and too far back in time for us to discern. Rather than a single doctrine or a single system of worship it is a broad confluence of ideas and attitudes. As it progresses great tributary streams flow into it. Four are of especial importance: the ancient Yoga tradition with the Sankhya philosophy to which it is linked; the Vedanta, the 'way of knowledge', stemming from the Upanishadic sages; the great Bhakti or devotional movement; and finally the Tantric tradition, with its emphasis upon the 'feminine' aspect of reality. These four elements, interacting with one another and woven together with the Vedic core, are the basis of Hinduism and they give this book its structure.

ONE

THE
Vedic
Background

It is difficult to exaggerate the importance of the Vedas within the Hindu tradition. All six of the *darshanas*, the 'viewpoints' or schools of Hindu philosophy, accept the authority of the Vedas. This is particularly true of the school which is today the most important and vigorous of all, the Vedanta, the very name of which proclaims its dependence on the Vedas. It is the Vedas, as we have seen, which mark the distinction between Hinduism and Buddhism: Hinduism acknowledges their authority, the Buddha did not.

If we turn to the social sphere it is the same story. The structure of Hindu society rests upon the Vedas. The Brahmins, the highest of the four classes into which society is divided, originally existed entirely for the Vedas – for their interpretation, their preservation and transmission, and for giving effect to their injunctions. The whole tremendous prestige of the Brahmin class throughout the course of Indian history derives from the Vedas.

So before we can understand very much about Indian society, or about Hindu thought and religion, it is important to have a clear idea of what the Vedas are and where their origins lie. For this we must step back nearly four thousand years.

The Aryan Entry into India[1]

The origins of the Vedas lie with the Aryan tribes who are thought to have entered northern India from the direction of Iran and Afghanistan some time between 2000 and 1200 B.C. Herdsmen and stockbreeders, expert in the care of cattle and the use of horses, the Aryans had probably been on the move, at least sporadically, for centuries.

Although they had no cities and were not much interested in settled farming, they were in some respects advanced. They were skilled in metallurgy and in the making of bronze weapons and tools. They already used stirrups. Their fast, two-horse war chariots were probably the equal of anything in the world at that time. Their religious ideas were complex, and the poetry in which they expressed them rich in striking imagery and dramatic power. In a passage from the Rig Veda, the celestial horse, Dadhikras, is imagined as an Aryan war horse:

> *Loudly the folk cry after him in battles,*
> *   as 'twere a thief who steals away a garment;*
> *Speeding to glory, or a herd of cattle,*
> *   even as a hungry falcon swooping downward.*
> *That strong Steed, victorious and faithful,*
> *   obedient with his body in the combat,*
> *Speeding straight on amid the swiftly pressing*
> *   hosts,*
> *   casts o'er his brows the dust he tosses upward.*
> *And at his thunder, like the roar of heaven,*
> *   those who attack tremble and are afraid.*[2]

For perhaps four or five hundred years the Aryans spread through northern India, moving gradually eastwards along the base of the Himalayas and south into the Ganges plain. A chain of kingdoms, often in conflict with one another, sprang up. The western half of the Ganges plain, and the region lying between the Ganges and the Yamuna rivers, became their heartland – Aryavarta, the land of the Aryans. Here, in what was one of the most fertile and productive lands of the world, their culture flourished. This region, which is today the state of Uttar Pradesh, is still the heart of India and the centre of political power.

The language of these invaders was Sanskrit, and it is a measure of their cultural impact that Sanskrit has ever since been the language of learning and religion in India.

Sanskrit and the Indo-Europeans

Sanskrit ceased to be the spoken language of northern India more than two thousand years ago. It became a privileged language, almost secret, in which the esoteric knowledge of the Brahmins was debated and preserved. Much later, Europeans had difficulty gaining access to it; but when, late in the eighteenth century, they did succeed they made an astonishing discovery: there were unmistakable signs of a relationship between Sanskrit and the languages of Europe.

A little later it was shown that Sanskrit was related to Greek, Latin, and ancient Iranian, and also to the Germanic, Celtic and Slav languages as well as certain others. When we speak of *yoga*, for example, we are really using our own word, *to yoke*, in the sense of harnessing or bringing together. A ship is *naus* in Sanskrit (our *navigation*); a god is *deva* (our *divinity*); knowledge is *jnana* (our *gnosis*); our word *three* is in Sanskrit *tri*; and the word for *father* is *pater* in both Latin and Greek, *pitar* in Sanskrit. There are hundreds of such correspondences, and they show that the Aryan tribes of India were linked in a great family, which came to be called Indo-European, with the successive waves of peoples – Greek, Italic, Celtic, German, Slav – who entered Europe in approximately the same early period. At some time in the remote past these peoples must have been in contact, perhaps united in a single race and living in a common homeland. The Vedic hymns have fascinated scholars, since they provide the earliest and best evidence of what the beliefs and way of life of this proto-Indo-European people may have been.

Just as there are linguistic links, so too are there links between the Vedic gods and those of Greek, Roman and German religion. One of the earliest gods of the Rig Veda is Dyaus Pitar ('Sky Father' or 'Heaven Father'), who is essentially the same deity and even bears the same name as the Greek Zeus (i.e. *Dyaus*) and the Roman Jupiter (i.e. *Ju*, a contraction of *Dyaus*, plus *piter*). Similarly, the Vedic god Varuna corresponds to the Greek Ouranos; and the Germanic god Thor (from whom our Thursday is named) and the Vedic god Indra, although their names differ, share a number of attributes which reveal their common origin.

These links are of more than scholarly interest, for they show us that the European psyche and that of India are not unconnected. When Christianity – a Semitic religion strongly focused on the idea of a unique personal God – was brought to Europe, it blossomed in somewhat contradictory fashion into a whole pantheon of angels and saints, each with his or her special abilities and area of concern. The old Indo-European pattern, seen in the gods of Greece and Rome, of the German and Celtic tribes, and of Vedic India, had reasserted itself. As the most famous of nineteenth-century Indologists, Max Muller, wrote: 'We all come from the East ... and in going to the East ... everybody ought to feel that he is going to his "old home" full of memories, if only he can read them.'[3]

The Indus Valley Civilization

But the Vedic religion is not the only source of Hinduism. When the first Aryan tribes entered India, one of the great early civilizations of the world had already flourished there for more than a thousand years. This was the Indus Valley civilization, best known for the two remarkable planned cities at Harappa and Mohenjo-daro. Dating back to at least 3000 B.C., it was comparable to the contemporary civilizations of Eygpt and Mesopotamia, and is known to have traded with the latter. Much about this civilization, including the reasons for its decline around 1600 B.C., remains a mystery. An earlier theory that it was destroyed by the invading Aryans has been largely abandoned.

We know little of the religion of the Indus civilization, for the small quantity of written material which has been found has not been deciphered. However, several facts emerge which point in the direction of the future Hindu synthesis. The most evident is a cult of the principle of male vitality, perhaps symbolized as, but not confined to, sexual power. This is seen in symbolic representations of the phallus made of polished stone (at a later period, called in India a *lingam*); frequent images of horned male animals such as the bull; and in small figures of a male god, sometimes with three faces, wearing a horned headdress and seated in what might be a Yoga posture. There is also interest in creatures associated with fertility such as snakes, and in what appears to be a sacred tree. In the cities the sanitation system is planned, elaborate, and unique for its time; and it seems to imply a concern with personal purity, social order, and ritual bathing. Even the stylized lingams suggest discipline and ascetic restraint rather than indulgent sexuality.[4]

More than a thousand years after the demise of the Indus civilization, we find these elements again as Hinduism emerges from the matrix of Vedic religion. In the worship of Shiva, who is not among the early Vedic deities (although Rudra, who later merged with Shiva, is), whose symbol is the *lingam* and whose animal companion is a white bull, it is possible that we see a partial reemergence of the male god of the Indus civilization.⁵ Snakes, called *nagas*, and sacred trees are prominent motives in popular Hinduism; while religious bathing and ideas of ritual purity are strongly marked characteristics of Hindu society.

Even so, we cannot be certain that all these features represent survivals from the Indus civilization. Throughout the rest of India many other peoples, some of whom have survived as the tribal groups of today, were to be found. As the Aryans moved eastwards, and down into the Ganges valley, they reported encounters with dark-skinned people whom they called *Dasyus*. Further south, many other peoples existed. Many popular and primitive elements must have entered Hinduism from these sources. One notable example may be the figure of Krishna Gopala, 'Krishna the cowherd' – as opposed to the princely Krishna of the epic literature. Another is the greater part of the Tantric tradition.

The Four Classes and the Caste System

A feature common to the various Indo-European peoples was a tendency to divide society into three classes. First in order of precedence came the priesthood (the Brahmins of India, the Flamens of Rome, the Druids of the Celts); second, the warriors and rulers (the Kshatriyas of India, sometimes also called Rajanyas); and third, the producers of economic wealth – farmers, merchants, and craftsmen (the Vaishyas). The Aryans brought this pattern with them into India, but once there, a fourth group was added. This consisted of the subjected indigenous peoples whom they called *Dasyus* or *Dasas*. They became the Shudras, the serfs and labourers. The fourfold scheme which resulted is described in the Rig Veda:

> *When they divided Purusha how many portions*
> *did they make?*
> *What do they call his mouth, his arms?*
> *What do they call his thighs and feet?*
> *The Brahmin was his mouth;*
> *Of both his arms was the Rajanya made.*
> *His thighs became the Vaishya;*
> *From his feet the Shudra was produced.*[6]

These, then, are the four classes or *varnas* into which the archetypal Man, *Purusha*, is divided. It is intended as a statement about the differing natures of men, and the natural form of society which results. The divisions were not hard and fast, and it was possible, though not usual, for a man to move from one *varna* into another. The high place accorded the Brahmins is a recognition of the value of the spiritual and intellectual side of man, as against political and military prowess (the Kshatriyas) and economic skills (the Vaishyas). Whatever may be the faults of the Brahmins in practice, the ideal they represent is a high one: the man whose whole life is dedicated to spiritual and intellectual pursuits, and to the preservation and transmission of the precious heritage of knowledge.

This division into four *varnas* or classes is still the basis of Hindu society, but in the course of time another principle, social and not religious in origin, has become confused with it. This is the principle of *jati* ('birth'), and it is this term, and not *varna*, which is correctly translated as caste.[7] Whereas the four *varnas*, the four great classes of Hindu society, have received the validation of the Vedas and are stable and unchanging, the *jatis* change in response to social conditions. During the upheavals of the eighteenth and nineteenth centuries large numbers of new castes came into being, so that the total number of castes is now more than three thousand. In this way the vast and shifting jigsaw puzzle of racial groupings, traditions, and inherited trades and professions which is Indian society is brought into a formal pattern of relationships.

The *jati* or caste system, purely social in nature, has been legitimized by the strategy of attaching it to the four classes or *varnas* (themselves legitimized by the Vedas), so that the *jatis* now appear as sub-divisions of the latter. The whole system has thus become attached in the popular mind, and in that of many foreign observers, to Hinduism, but in reality it has little to do with it. The caste system is a social phenomenon masquerading as religion.

The Vedic Literature

The word *Veda* means 'a body of knowledge' and the Vedas, like the Bible, are a compilation of many texts. Rather than regarding them as a book, we should do better to think of them as a library. The different parts of the Vedas have accumulated over a span of time even longer than that of the Bible – perhaps as much as two thousand years, or according to some Indian estimates even more.

These texts were not written but were passed down orally. The Vedas were precious and powerful. They were the key to what was most important in life. They were entrusted to the Brahmins, and to commit them to writing would have been to betray that trust. Once something is written it exists in a material form. It then becomes open to all sorts of vicissitudes; anyone may get hold of it, use it for their own ends, misinterpret it or corrupt it. Only in recent centuries has this attitude been relaxed. Before that the whole mass of the Vedas was transmitted orally, learnt by heart by the Brahmins, different families and schools specializing in different parts of it. This was done with great accuracy – we know this, for the tradition of oral transmission is still maintained in India. Hence the Veda is called *shruti*, 'that which is heard', that which has been passed down by immemorial tradition.

There are four Vedas, called the Rig, Sama, Yajur and Atharva Vedas. Of these the Rig Veda, containing the great songs of praise addressed to the ancient gods, is the oldest and easily the most important. The Sama Veda is for the most part a different arrangement of the same material, made for specific liturgical purposes; the Yajur Veda contains the sacrificial formulas, and is of rather specialized interest; and the Atharva Veda, which was added to the other three at a later date, contains spells and incantations and appears to derive from the level of folk religion. From our present point of view, it is the Rig Veda which is of interest, and the other three may be set aside.

To each Veda there are four distinct layers of text, accumulated during different epochs and corresponding to successive periods of religious development. The earliest level consists of those texts called Samhitas. These are the core of the four Vedas, the original collection of verses round which the rest has grown. Thus the Rig Veda Samhita (usually referred to simply as the Rig Veda), which sung the praises of the old gods, contains what is probably the oldest of all the Vedic material. Then come the Brahmanas, named like the *varna* or class which gave them birth.[8] These are commentaries and instructions for the sacrifices made to the gods. The last two levels are the Aranyakas and the Upanishads, but since the former are transitional between the Brahmanas and the Upanishads and do not have a strongly marked character they may be ignored for present purposes. The Upanishads, on the other hand, are of great importance. Thus we have in effect three levels of text corresponding to three distinct phases of Vedic religion.

The Rig Veda

The earliest phase of Vedic religion is that corresponding to the original core, the Samhitas, especially that of the Rig Veda. The Rig Veda Samhita is a collection of 1028 poems; hymns of praise and petition directed to the *devas*, the gods of the Aryan pantheon. They are arranged in ten books, perhaps originating as the collections of particular Brahmin families, each generation preserving and passing on the old songs and perhaps adding a few new ones. The hymns were sung or chanted according to exact rules, as part of the sacrificial ritual. Just how old these songs are nobody knows with certainty, but there is agreement that they are extremely ancient. Western scholars tend to date them between 1500 and 1200 B.C., the period in which the Aryans are thought to have entered India. A few songs could go back to a time even before the Aryans had reached India.[9] The Rig Veda Samhita has been called with some justification 'the oldest book in the world'.

The songs of the Rig Veda are difficult to interpret but it is clear that the cosmos is controlled by *devas*, gods. Although their existence is far superior to that of men they are not absolute realities: they, like men, are ultimately mortal, a part of the existent universe. The *devas*, although they can and do come in contact with men, are beings existing on another plane. Through them the primal divine energies and intelligence flow down to the level of material existence, and by them existence is directed and controlled.

Although the *devas* are conceived in personal terms, the ultimate reality behind them is not. More fundamental and real than the gods is the divine law called *rita*. *Rita* is the order inherent in all that is, the harmony integrating the cosmos, the law of the universe. Once again, this idea goes back to the common Indo-European heritage.[10]

11

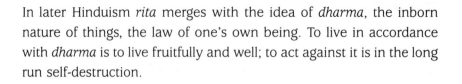
In later Hinduism *rita* merges with the idea of *dharma*, the inborn nature of things, the law of one's own being. To live in accordance with *dharma* is to live fruitfully and well; to act against it is in the long run self-destruction.

There are many passages in the Rig Veda which remain of the greatest importance to Hindus. There is for example the famous hymn called the *Purusha Shukta*, which is still recited every day in millions of Hindu households; and another verse, known from its metre as the *Gayatri*, which is considered to contain the entire Veda in a compressed form.[11] Also important, in that it broaches one of the great questions of metaphysics and anticipates much later Hindu thought, is the famous Creation Hymn of the Rig Veda. In it the poet meditates on how, from the unconditioned Absolute, a conditioned universe can come into being:

> *Then was not non-existent nor existent:*
> *There was no realm of air, no sky beyond it.*
> *That One Thing, breathless, breathed by its own*
>   *nature:*
> *Apart from it was nothing whatsoever.*
>
> *Darkness there was: at first concealed in darkness*
> *This All was indiscriminated chaos.*
> *All that existed then was void and formless:*
> *By the power of concentration* (tapas) *that came*
>   *forth.*
>
> *Then in the beginning Desire arose;*
> *Desire, the primal seed and germ of Mind.*
> *Sages who searched with their heart's thought,*
> *Discovered the existent's kinship in the non-existent.*

Who verily knows and who can here declare it,
Whence it was born and whence came this
   creation?
The Gods are later than this world's production;
Who knows, then, whence its being?

He, the first origin of this creation,
Whether he formed it, or did not form it,
Whose eye, in highest heaven, controls this world,
He verily knows it – or perhaps he knows it
   not.[12]

The problems with which this poem wrestles are still the problems of philosophy, whether in the East or the West. From other hymns scholars have been able to reconstruct several of the original myths which the Aryans brought with them into India, but the true meaning of the early Vedic religion, and the spiritual insights it embodied, are more difficult to determine. What can be said is that it is unlikely that the real content was confined to the surface meaning of the texts, or even to their immediately apparent symbolic meaning. Gods such as Savitri or Surya (two aspects of the Sun), or Agni (Fire), do not simply represent natural phenomena; they are spiritual principles, aspects of supreme reality, which stand behind the natural phenomena and give rise to them. It was not so much the physical Sun which was valued and worshipped, but the principle of light, and therefore of consciousness, which it manifests – the Sun within the heart, which lights up and endows with beauty and meaning the entire world.[13] This understanding of the cosmos has carried through from the Rig Veda to the present day. A contemporary scholar has written: It is not just a superstitious remnant if today Hindus offer praises and prayers to the rising sun at the time of their morning prayer. Many a modern Indian among those sun

13

worshippers knows about the physical properties of the sun, its surface temperature, and its chemical composition. Worship is not addressed to the astronomical body, nor to a symbolic idea, but to the *surya-deva*, the metaphysical reality through which an aspect of the supreme reality becomes relevant for people.'[14]

TWO

THE SACRIFICE
and the
Upanishads

Running through the Hindu tradition from the time of the early Vedic hymns to the present day we find two perennial themes. The first is a concern with the order of the cosmos and its maintenance. It finds its expression in forms of ritual activity and the concept of the Brahmin priest. The second is a search for personal salvation or *moksha* ('release'). It leads to philosophical speculation and mysticism, and to the concept of the *rishi* and in later times the Guru. The first of these themes finds its fullest expression in the Brahmanas, the second in the Upanishads.

The Brahmanas

The Brahmanas are the texts corresponding to the middle period of Vedic religion. As the sacred verses forming the Samhitas were passed down there grew around them a layer of commentary which became in time the Brahmanas. While the precise wording of the Samhita texts was carefully preserved, variations in this accompanying material grew up among different schools. In this way several different Brahmanas came to be attached to each of the Samhitas and the Brahmana literature grew to massive proportions. The Brahmanas represent a time when the influence of the Brahmin caste was at its height, and the Vedic religion was tending to harden into a fixed form. Western scholars usually date them between 900 and 500 B.C. – Indians much earlier – but in any case it is clear that they represent the interpretations of an altogether later age than that of the Samhitas.

The Idea of the Sacrifice

The Brahmanas are concerned with the balance of cosmic forces. The key to maintaining this was the sacrifices. By sacrifices to the gods, regularly performed by the Brahmin priests, the cosmic order is maintained and the individual on whose behalf the sacrifice is made is rewarded by the gods either in this life or in heaven. In the Vedic period images of the deities were not made and there were no temples. An altar, conforming to a strict symbolic pattern, was constructed in the open for each occasion, and the post to which the sacrificial animal was tied was regarded as the cosmic axis linking the lower and upper worlds. There were different sacrifices, ranging from great ones such as the *ashva-medha* or Horse Sacrifice, which a king might perform and which took many months and great resources to prepare, to common daily oblations using such items as rice, honey, butter and curds. The gods, drawn to the altar by the songs of praise and chanting of the priests, received the food and other gifts through the medium of the sacrificial fire. It was believed that the gods, whose expression lay in the great energies of the cosmos, expended their strength in the maintenance of the universe; through the regular performance of the sacrifices they in turn were maintained and their powers replenished.

The religion of sacrifice often appears in the not very exalted light of a bargain with the gods, yet this is really the decadence of the original idea. Behind the sacrifices of the Vedic religion lies a recognition of the fact that the whole universe is in itself and of its very nature a vast and continuous sacrifice. The world of plants sacrifices itself to animals, and animals to one another and to men. Our own physical being has become possible through the sacrifices of our ancestors, and it is our self-sacrifice which sustains our children. The five elements of the material world – ether, air, fire, water, earth –

and the *devas* who control them are engaged in continual sacrifice one to another: water erodes earth, earth absorbs water, etc. The Supreme Reality sacrifices its own nature by the very act of coming under limitation in the manifest universe – even though in some way, and from another point of view, its transcendent perfection is never lost. The Vedic sacrifice is the microcosmic representation of the never-ending destruction and renewal of all life and matter. It is sacrifice which sustains the world; which is the very nature of the world. Man is part of this process, and he must give back as well as draw from it.

In the eyes of the Brahmins the whole of existence was linked together in a series of correspondences to which the sacrifice was the key. The Vedic fire-altar was understood as an image of the universe, and the sacrifice as a disguised sacrifice of oneself: the heart is the altar, the outer man the offering, and the purified inner man the flame.[1] A verse in the Rig Veda describes the sacrifice of Purusha, the Cosmic Man, likening the elements of the sacrifice to the seasons:

> *When Gods prepared the sacrifice with Purusha*
> *as their offering,*
> *Its oil was spring, the holy gift was autumn,*
> *Summer was the wood.*
> *They balmed as victim on the grass Purusha,*
> *Born in earliest time ...*[2]

Thus, properly understood, the whole of man's life is a continuous sacrifice. The only question is whether one joins willingly and consciously in the great ongoing process of mutual sacrifice which is the universe, recognizing and affirming one's unity with the whole, or whether one fails to understand and takes part only as its unwilling victim.

18

The Crisis of Vedic Religion

Although there are many injunctions in the Brahmanas asserting the need to know the inner meaning of the sacrifices, it appears that this was increasingly obscured by the idea that the expertise of the Brahmin priests could unfailingly produce the material or heavenly result sought for. It came to be believed that the gods had no choice but to reward the sacrificer as requested. If the correct sacrifices were offered at the right time and place, the rituals performed and the sacred hymns chanted with meticulous precision – if a single word or movement was out of place the entire performance became ineffective – the god concerned was then virtually constrained to deliver the desired result, for such was the order of things.

In this way great prestige and influence accrued to the Brahmins, on whose expertise all that was most important in life and even after life depended. But the success was bought at a price. The original meaning and spiritual effectiveness of the sacrifice was obscured as the sacrificial system declined towards a mechanical ritualism. As the sense of a spiritual vacuum grew, a wave of religious restiveness and seeking seems to have swept across northern India. Even the objectives for which the sacrifices were performed came to seem, to those who thought more deeply about them, of a limited value. The sojourn in Indra's heaven would eventually come to an end, when the religious capital acquired through the sacrifices was used up. Whereas in the oldest parts of the Veda the idea of reincarnation is not present, it now came to be believed that one would then return to the earth and the whole process would start anew. A text from a much later period, the Vishnu Purana, sets out the argument in precise form:

*If you suppose that the objects to be effected by
sacrificial rites, performed according to the rules
of the Rik, Yajur, and Sama Vedas, be the great
end of life, attend to what I have to say. Any
effect which is produced through the causality of
earth partakes of the character of its origin, and
consists, itself, of clay: so, any act performed by
perishable agents, such as fuel, clarified butter,
and Kusha grass, must, itself, be but of temporary
efficacy. The great end of life (or truth) is
considered, by the wise, to be eternal: but it
would be transient, if it were accomplished
through transitory things.*[3]

Yet human life necessarily entails suffering. Even the most fortunate
life is driven by desires, and desire implies a want, a pain: 'Verily,
the embodied self is held by pleasure and pain. Surely, there is no
cessation of pleasure and pain for one who is embodied.'[4] Could
there be, then, beyond this life, beyond even the heaven of Indra,
another order of existence? One that was stable, unchanging, and
therefore ultimately real? One that was free from desire, and therefore free of pain? One that would give a joy that did not end? In this
way the seeds of a great renewal of religious life were sown.

The old Vedic religion seemed to have lost its way and a profound
crisis overtook the religious life of India. It was to last several centuries, and in its heat the new synthesis that was Hinduism was
forged. This was also the context in which the Buddha, breaking
altogether with the Vedic tradition, pioneered a new path to salvation; and in which Mahavira established the Jain religion. New ideas,
notably that of *ahimsa*, the non-injury of all beings, sweep through
religious life. Ideas and techniques of salvation rooted in the

autochthonous traditions of India start to re-emerge. A little later a new theism begins to stir, and gods and *avataras* unknown to Vedic religion appear. Some of the earliest signs of these changes are found in the Upanishads.

The Upanishads

It has been said that in the songs of the Rig Veda it is the poet who speaks, in the Brahmanas the priest, and in the Upanishads the philosopher and the mystic. Unlike much of the earlier Vedic literature, and across a span of two and a half millennia, the Upanishads speak to us in a direct and immediate manner. In their pages we find ourselves in what seems a different world from the carefully structured ritualism of the Brahmanas. In place of a claim to settled knowledge and an infallible method, the mood is one of eager enquiry and discovery. The Brahmin caste still plays the leading role but it is no longer the exclusive arbiter of religious life.

Even in the earliest Upanishads we find Brahmins coming for instruction to the class below them, the Kshatriyas. We find a young boy, Satyakama Jabala, who admits that his mother does not know who his father was; he is accepted as a Brahmin and worthy to receive the inner knowledge simply on account of his truthfulness. And we find women such as Maitreyi and the erudite Gargi engaged in keen debate with renowned Brahmin sages. In another Upanishad we read that the sacrificial methods are fragile and perishable, and that those who practise them, thinking themselves wise and learned, are deluded 'like the blind led by the blind'. Such things were inconceivable in the earlier period.

The change from the thought of the Brahmanas to that of the Upanishads has been called 'probably the most remarkable event in the history of philosophic thought'. Yet it would be wrong to see the Upanishads as representing a break with the Vedic past, and the same writer has also called them 'the culmination of the intellectual achievement of a great epoch'.[5] Although the Upanishads mark the transition from the old Vedic religion to Hinduism proper, they also form part of the Vedas and are deeply rooted in the ancient tradition.

The word *Upanishad* means 'sitting down near'; i.e. sitting down near a teacher so as to hear his words from his own lips. What is implied is the personal transmission of spiritual knowledge, and the Upanishads have the character of an inner teaching originating on the margins of the old Vedic religion. Such teaching was transmitted orally by the *rishis* or sages, often men living in forest retreats. Given little by little and as a precious gift, it was imparted only to those who were thought worthy, and indeed capable, of grasping its real import. These teachings were treasured, memorized and passed on in the same way as the earlier parts of the Vedas. Thus the sayings of the great forest *rishis* were preserved, and the Upanishads became part of the Vedic tradition.

Ultimate Reality – Brahman and Atman

Throughout the Vedic literature we find people asking again and again, what is it that lies behind existence, what is the unchanging reality on which all else must rest?

I, unknowing, ignorant, here
Ask the wise sages for the sake of knowledge:
What was That One, in the form of the unborn,
Who established these six worlds?[6]

Various names are attached to the mysterious That One: *Vishvakarman*, 'the All-Doer'; *Purusha*, 'the Person', the cosmic Man; *Prajapati*, 'the Lord of Creatures'; or simply *Ka*, 'the Who?', but it is only in the Upanishads that the answer is probed for in a persistent and penetrating manner. The Upanishads record the thoughts of many different sages, but the word used for the ultimate reality is usually *Brahman*. We have already met variants of this word in the terms Brahmin and Brahmana. In the earlier parts of the Veda Brahman means that which is 'great' or 'vast', often the power inherent in the sacred hymns and the sacrifices. In the Upanishads this concept is broadened so that Brahman becomes the power underlying the whole of existence, the source of being, the one ultimate reality: 'Verily, all this universe is Brahman. From Him do all things originate, into Him do they dissolve and by Him are they sustained.'[7]

This, however, is only to name the mystery. The Upanishads try to do more. Rather than searching for the solution in the macrocosm they turn inwards. They approach the question through a second idea, that of Atman. The Atman is that awareness which is the inner Self and being of man, and of all other creatures. It is awareness itself, pure consciousness – not consciousness *of* anything, but consciousness in itself, unconditioned by any object. It never changes; it is like a steady beam of light. It is what makes everything else possible, for it is on this ground of pure awareness that the world and everything in it appears to us. This Self or Atman, then, the inner consciousness, is that Reality which underlies life and all

23

of manifestation, and it is therefore identical with Brahman. The Aitareya Upanishad lists all that lives in the universe – the gods, the five elements, the creatures born of eggs, of wombs, of moisture and of the earth, horses, cattle, men, elephants, and all the creatures that there are. It then tells us:

> All these have Consciousness as the giver of their reality; all these are impelled by Consciousness; the universe has Consciousness as its eye, and Consciousness is its end. Consciousness is Brahman.[8]

In the Chandogya Upanishad we read the same thing: 'That which is the finest essence – this whole world has that as its soul. That is Reality. That is Atman. That art thou.'[9] These words, repeated nine times in the text, are the core of the Upanishadic message: *Tat tvam asi*, 'That thou art' – Brahman, the ultimate reality underlying the universe, and Atman, the innermost reality of every man and every living thing, are identical. Another text says, 'You are the Indestructible; you are the Unshaken; you are the very essence of life'.[10]

The Two Birds on the One Tree

Although it is our very self, Atman or Brahman is not something we can know in the normal sense of discursive knowledge. All that can be said of it, the Upanishads tell us, is that it is *neti, neti*, 'not this, not this'. It is not, and it can never be, an object of knowledge because it is prior to knowledge, being the ground upon which the whole process of knowing takes place:

> *That which man does not comprehend with the*
> *mind, that by which, they say, the mind is*
> *encompassed, know that to be Brahman and not*
> *what people worship as an object. That which*
> *man does not see with the eyes, that by which*
> *man perceives the activities of the eye, know*
> *that alone to be Brahman and not what people* Kena 1.6-1.7
> *worship as an object.*[11]

> *It is not coarse, not fine, not short, not long …*
> *Verily, O Gargi, if one performs sacrifices and*
> *worship and undergoes austerity in this world for*
> *many thousands of years, but without knowing*
> *that Imperishable, limited indeed is that work of*
> *his. Verily, O Gargi, he who departs from this*
> *world without knowing that Imperishable is* Brihad - 3-8 (8-10).
> *pitiable.*[12]

Thus there are two realms: first, that of empirical existence and ordinary knowing, the world of 'name and form' as the Upanishads often call it; and behind it, that quite different order of reality to which the mind does not have access and which is Brahman – or, when spoken of in relation to man, Atman. This idea of two orders of reality existing within man had existed in embryonic form within Vedic thought from a very early time. In the Rig Veda we read that:

> *Two Birds with fair wings, knit with bonds of*
> *   friendship,*
> *In the same sheltering tree have found a refuge.*
> *One of the twain eats the sweet Figtree's fruitage;*
> *The other, eating not, regardeth only.*[13]

25

WAY of

As both the Upanishadic sages and the later thinkers of the Advaita Vedanta school understood, these two birds seated in the Tree of Life are the Self or Atman (the bird which 'eating not, regardeth only') and the empirical, day-to-day self of man, the individual which experiences or 'eats' the fruit of life. It is this latter self, the Indian term for which is *jiva*, with which we mistakenly identify, and this is the error from which all others, and all sufferings, arise. In a later chapter we will see how this idea was developed by the Vedanta.

25.10.4.

THREE

HINDU GODS:
The Trimurti

The idea of Brahman put forward in the Upanishads is not one which can satisfy the demands of the mind. The 'knowing' of which the Upanishads speak is of a different order. Brahman-Atman can only be 'known' by identity with it, by direct intuition. It lies outside the duality of subject and object and cannot be spoken of in terms of relations. It is *Nirguna*, 'without qualities' of any sort, for these would limit its absolute nature. Since the mind deals only with relations and qualities the reality of Brahman must remain forever outside its grasp.

It is therefore not surprising that in the period succeeding the Upanishads the idea of Brahman came to be clothed in forms which the human mind and the imagination can grasp. The result was a vigorous development of theism, during which the gods and goddesses which today characterize Hinduism assumed much of their character. Many of these deities have Vedic origins, but they are now thought of not in relation to the sacrifice, but as varied expressions of the one all-pervasive Reality. The Vishnu Purana, a text coming towards the end of this process (about the fourth century A.D.), ennunciates the principle in a striking passage:

regarding nature of God.

> *The blaze of fire burning on one spot diffuses*
> *light and heat around. So the world is nothing*
> *more than the manifested energy of the supreme*
> *Brahman. And, inasmuch as the light and heat*
> *are stronger or feebler as we are near to the fire*
> *or far from it, so the energy of the supreme is*
> *more or less intense in the beings that are less or*
> *more remote from him. Brahma, Vishnu, and*
> *Shiva are the most powerful energies of god.*
> *Next to them are the inferior deities; then, the*
> *attendant spirits; then, men; then, animals, birds,*

*insects, plants; each becoming more and more
feeble, as they are further from their primitive
source.*[1]

Thus Brahman and all the gods and goddesses, as well as man and
everything else in the universe, are parts of a continuum. The Hindu
deities are not viewed as separate and rival powers, but as different
functions, different aspects, different ways of understanding and
approaching the one Reality. When Brahman is considered in this
way He is said to be *Saguna*, 'with qualities', and is thought of as
revealing Himself to those who turn to Him. This is the basis for the
many different gods and goddesses, any of whom may be considered as the Supreme Reality. The ancient principle, *to what is One,
sages give many a title*, still holds sway; and by considering the
Supreme Reality in different ways we can build up a more rounded
picture than would otherwise be possible. However, some of these
forms are closer to the central functions of that Reality than others,
and chief amongst these are the Trimurti or 'Three Forms' of
Brahman – the gods Brahma, Vishnu and Shiva. But before we turn
to these, it will be useful to consider some of the principles used in
the representation of Hindu deities.

Hindu Imagery

Perhaps the first thing to strike a Western observer about the Hindu
deities is the multiplicity of limbs they display. Nineteenth-century
writers, brought up on Greek sculpture, found this grotesque and
inexplicable. Yet the reason why the Hindu deities are represented
in this way is very simple: it is to show that they *are* gods, that they
differ from human beings and have more and greater powers than
they. Thus Vishnu is usually shown with four arms, but his *avataras*

or incarnations, Rama and Krishna, who have human forms, are invariably represented with two.

The use of symbolism extends to every detail of the image of a deity. Each god or goddess holds certain objects – the discus of Vishnu, the sword of Durga, the two lotuses of Lakshmi – and to these a precise meaning attaches. Each of the main deities is associated with an animal or bird, upon which he or she is often pictured as riding. This is the god's *vahana* or 'bearer', and is a further way of symbolizing the dominant quality of the deity. Thus Vishnu has the solar bird Garuda, Shiva the white bull Nandi, Ganesha a rat, Durga a lion. Finally, there are standard gestures called *mudras* which the gods display, and which also form an important feature of Indian dancing. Such gestures are believed to carry power. The most frequently seen are the *abhaya mudra*, which has the meaning 'fear-not', and the *varada mudra* or 'boon-bestowing' gesture.

In such ways every aspect of the image of a deity is made meaningful. It is not simply a beautiful object, but a complex statement, a product of the intellect: 'The image of a deity is merely a group of symbols, and no element of its form should be the fruit of the inventiveness of an image maker. Every peculiarity of the attitude, of the expression, or of the ornaments is of significance and is intended as a fit object for meditation.'[2]

Let us see how these principles are applied to the Trimurti, the three great gods who are Brahman seen in relation to the three phases of the world process. They are, as we have seen, Brahma (the masculine and personalized form of the word Brahman), Vishnu and Shiva. Brahma is the creator-god; Vishnu the preserver of the universe; and Shiva that principle which, turning away from the world, transcends it and in this sense brings about its destruction.

Figure 1. Brahma, the Creator

Brahma, The Creator

Brahma is represented with four faces. These are turned towards the four directions of space, for it is he who has brought the whole extent of the universe into being. With his four arms Brahma holds a rosary, representing time; a water pot – since water, being formless, symbolizes the potential for creation; a sacrificial instrument, for it is by sacrifice that the world came into being; and finally a book, for as the Creator he makes possible all knowledge – Brahma, in fact, is sometimes equated with the human mind and the power of thought.

The consort of Brahma is the goddess Vac ('speech'), also called Saraswati. She is the beautiful goddess of speech with its immense power; the bestower of intelligence who protects all the arts and sciences. His *vamana* or bearer is a *hamsa*, the wild goose whose home is in the lakes of Central Asia beyond the Himalayas, symbol of the pilgrim soul which will one day take flight to its true home.

Brahma furnishes an example of the processes of change in Hinduism. In all of India only one temple remains dedicated to this once great god. Two developments have brought this about. First, a wide, but not universal, acceptance of the idea that the world we experience has only a provisional reality and so is not created in any absolute sense. And second, the belief that the supreme God (especially when thought of as Shiva) has a feminine counterpart, his Shakti or 'power', through which all activity takes place. The worship of Shakti – or Mahadevi, 'the Great Goddess' – as the creative principle bringing the universe into being, has made Brahma redundant. In a later chapter we shall see that it has become the third most important cult within Hinduism, ceding place only to the worship of Shiva and of Vishnu.

Figure 2. Vishnu, the Preserver

Vishnu, The Preserver

Vishnu has grown in importance as Brahma has declined, and he is for a very large section of Hindus the supreme deity, God himself. The word Vishnu means 'the one who pervades', and Vishnu is thought of both as immanent in the world, and as the transcendent Reality. He is represented as dark blue in colour, like infinite space. This is also the colour of the rain clouds which at the start of the monsoon bring relief and joy to the parched land – rain descending from the heavens to give life to earth is in many cultures a symbol of grace. Vishnu is most often represented standing upright in a frontal pose. This pillar-like stance, also common in images of the Buddha, is a reference to Vishnu's role as the Sustainer of the Worlds. It echoes an ancient idea: that of the pillar of the universe, the spiritual axis running vertically through the various levels of existence and supporting the universe.

In his four arms – representing his universal sovereignty – Vishnu usually holds a conch, discus, mace, and lotus flower. The conch shell stands for Vishnu's role as the origin of existence. It is found in water, which as we have seen symbolizes the potential for creation before manifestation. A conch shell is often blown at the start of Hindu ceremonies, and its deep, powerful note is associated with the primeval sound, OM, which is said to contain all of creation in potential.[3]

The discus or *chakra* stands for the Cosmic Mind, which brings the multiple forms of the universe into being (the discus spins round ceaselessly in some representations, though this cannot be conveyed in sculpture): 'In his hand Vishnu holds, in the form of his discus, the mind, whose thoughts fly swifter than the winds.'[4] In Vaishnaism (the cult of Vishnu), the world is almost always seen in positive terms, and here the mind is viewed positively as an instrument of liberation: 'The prodigious power of the mind can destroy all forms of ignorance, hence the discus is the fearful weapon that cuts off the heads of all demons, of all errors.'[5] The mace is the power of time which Vishnu wields, destroying all that opposes it.[6] Finally, the lotus is the beautiful world which arises from the being of the Supreme Reality. Just as a lotus is rooted obscurely in the muddy depths and rises to float upon the surface, an image of purity opened to the light of the sun, so too the world arises mysteriously from the depths of the unmanifest and opens itself to the all-pervading light of consciousness.

Shiva, Lord of the Dance

Hindu iconography has crystallized in a few images of especially great power. Shiva Nataraja, Shiva 'Lord of the Dance', is one. It is an image of the activity of God – of the primal rhythmic energy which animates the universe, issuing from the still centre of Reality.[7]

As in the case of Vishnu, Shiva, when viewed as the supreme God, includes within himself all three functions of the Trimurti. Once again, he has four arms to denote universality, and in his upper right hand he holds a small drum. This is Sound, which corresponds to creation. In the Hindu view, it is through sound – thought of either as speech *(Vac)* and hence intelligence and the power to differentiate, or, still more fundamentally, simply as vibration – that everything that is comes into being. Sound is vibration, and all matter may be said to consist of vibrations. Hearing is our last contact with the world as we lose consciousness, and our first as we regain it. The rhythm which Shiva beats out on this drum is the rhythm at the heart of the universe – the rhythm of the celestial bodies, the

35

Figure 3. Shiva Nataraja, Lord of the Dance

rhythm of creation and dissolution, the rhythm of each life. It is to this primordial rhythm that Shiva dances and all things come into being and pass away.

Symmetrically opposed to the drum, Shiva balances upon the palm of his upper left hand a flame. This symbolizes the destruction of the world, and represents Shiva in his most characteristic aspect as the Destroyer of Forms. It is the flame of the cremation ground, symbol of those who 'die' to the world. In India, those who have renounced the world wear robes of this colour. But by the same token, the flame is the symbol of transformation, for it is the form only which is destroyed and the Reality which animates it (and seemed to be limited by it) finds release. Far from being negative, the flame which Shiva bears aloft is supremely positive. It is the flame in which the limitations of individualized existence are burned up as the purified spirit rises into the Infinite.

Yet the Dance of Shiva is all-embracing, and it includes the processes of life as well as those of transcendence. As the two upper arms of Shiva Nataraja symbolize creation and destruction – or manifestation and release – so the lower right hand is raised in the divine gesture 'fear-not' *(abhaya mudra)*, the gesture of benignity, preservation and protection. Here we see Shiva absorbing the function of Vishnu. About this arm (or sometimes round Shiva's neck) a cobra is twined: snakes, associated since ancient times with the earth and with fertility, are never far distant when God is thought of in relation to the continuity of life.

The three arms we have considered so far represent the three aspects of the cosmic process, creation, maintenance, and transformation or dissolution. These three functions are linked to the fate of the individual by the fourth of Shiva's arms, the lower left arm, which swings across the body and points downwards. This gesture, called *gaja-hasta-mudra*, is likened to the trunk or 'hand' of an elephant and so reminds the Hindu worshipper of Shiva's son, the benign and popular elephant-headed god, Ganesha. Ganesha is the Remover of Obstacles, and the *gaja-hasta-mudra* indicates the mercy and favour of God, who in this way shows us the path to release. It is directed to Shiva's left foot, raised in the movement of the dance: the aspirant believes that by directing his devotion to this foot Shiva's grace can be attracted, and the release symbolized by the flame he holds aloft realized. While the left foot shows the positive aspect of *moksha* the right foot is its negative aspect. It tramples upon a small sprawling dwarf. He is 'the man Forgetfulness' – forgetfulness both of God and of our own real nature. The entire image of Shiva Nataraja rests upon this essential conquest of the principle of Ignorance; it is the base upon which all else is erected.

Shiva Nataraja is especially associated with South India, and the meanings we have explored are summarized in an old Tamil text addressed to Shiva:

> *O my Lord, Thy hand holding the sacred drum*
> *has made and ordered the heavens and earth*
> *and other worlds and innumerable souls. Thy*
> *lifted hand protects both the conscious and*
> *unconscious order of Thy creation. All these*
> *worlds are transformed by Thy hand bearing*
> *fire. Thy sacred foot, planted on the ground,*
> *gives an abode to the tired soul struggling in*
> *the toils of causality. It is Thy lifted foot that*
> *grants eternal bliss to those that approach Thee.*[8]

These then are the limbs of the dancing Lord Shiva, flashing in the unending dance of the cosmos as his heels stamp out the great and small rhythms of the universe. Above them, perfectly balanced, is the head, with its long hair spread out behind by the movement of the dance. It would take too long to go into the multiple symbolism of this hair, twined in which there is usually a wreathing serpent, a skull, the mermaid figure of the Ganges, a crescent moon, and a wreath of Cassia leaves. But what we must notice is the face of Shiva. Poised centrally above the flying limbs, displaying no movement, impassive, mask-like, it is so detached that it seems almost to float. Only a faint smile plays across the lips. It is the face of the Great Yogi, he who knows the inner secret of manifestation. The contrast between the still face and the flying hair and limbs is that between the inner Self and the ever-active mind and its world. Here, utterly still at the centre of the dance, is the inner witness, the omnipresent Self, the unmoved Mover, the still point at the centre of the ever-changing world.

Much more could be written regarding the meaning of the images of Vishnu and Shiva and of the many other gods and goddesses of Hinduism, but enough has been said to give some idea of the principles involved and of the complexity of these forms.

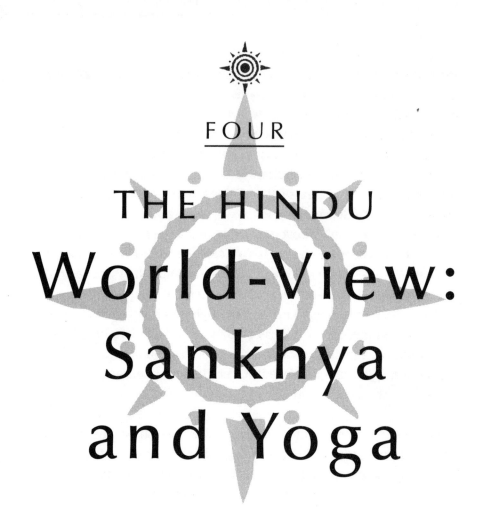

FOUR

THE HINDU
World-View: Sankhya and Yoga

Hinduism derives much of its unity from a characteristic world-view, which is widely shared by its different schools. Belief in rebirth and in the law of Karma are two aspects of this to which we will turn in a later chapter. Underlying these beliefs is a vision of an ordered, rhythmic universe: the world-process is cyclical in nature; the universe comes into being and passes away according to a regular pattern, like that of day and night or of in-breathing and out-breathing. The pattern has no beginning and no end. It is simply the nature of things.

Cyclical Time

We have seen that the Dance of Shiva is, among other things, a representation of the rhythmic nature of the universe. The universe is not something which is created; it is closer to a natural process, almost an organism. It arises out of the being of the Supreme Reality, not for any reason, but simply because it is the nature of that Reality that it should do so. Having come into being, the universe is maintained for a while, and at last sinks back into the unmanifest state within the Supreme Reality from which it came. There it will lie dormant, like a hidden seed, until it emerges once more at the commencement of a future cycle.

Such a grand cycle, involving an immense vista of time, is called a *Kalpa*. Within these great cycles are many lesser cycles, called *Mahayugas*. A Mahayuga is said to last for 4,320,000 years, and it has within it four ages or *Yugas*. These are not unlike the Gold, Silver, Bronze and Iron ages of classical antiquity. Each is shorter, and worse in quality, than the age which preceded it. The Kali Yuga, the last of the four, extends for 432,000 years; the age before it for double that period, and the two earlier ages for three times and four times that period. Thus we obtain the total of 4,320,000 years – one Mahayuga or sub-cycle of the world's existence. The same sequence is then repeated again and again. One thousand Mahayugas constitute a Kalpa (described as a 'day of Brahma', the god responsible for the manifestation of the world), and at the end of this period the entire universe reverts to the unmanifest state from which it came forth. A similar period of another one thousand Mahayugas now elapses ('a night of Brahma'), and then the whole process commences anew with a fresh emanation of the universe from the being of Vishnu.

The Present Age – The Kali Yuga

Hindus believe that we are at present in the Kali Yuga, the last and darkest of the four ages, which commenced at the end of Krishna's appearance upon the earth. The most famous description of the Kali Yuga is given in the Vishnu Purana, which paints a gloomy picture:

> *The observance of caste, order, and institutes will not prevail in the Kali age; nor will that of the ceremonial enjoined by the Sama, Rig, and Yajur Vedas. Marriages in this age, will not be conformable to the ritual; nor will the rules that connect the spiritual preceptor and his disciple be in force. The laws that regulate the conduct of husband and wife will be disregarded; and oblations to the gods with fire no longer be offered . . . Accumulated treasures will be expended on dwellings. The minds of men will be wholly occupied in acquiring wealth; and wealth*

will be spent solely on selfish gratifications.
Women will follow their inclinations, and be ever
fond of pleasure. Men will fix their desires upon
riches, even though dishonestly acquired . . .
In the Kali age, Maitreya, men, corrupted by
unbelievers, will refrain from adoring Vishnu,
the lord of sacrifice, the creator and lord of all,
and will say: 'Of what authority are the Vedas?
What are gods, or Brahmins?'[1]

Yet in spite of this dark picture, the Kali age is said to have its own advantages. First, it is the herald of a great renewal, for once the depths of the Kali Yuga have been plumbed, and all that is lowest and worst in humanity has found expression, a new Golden Age will dawn at the commencement of a fresh Mahayuga. Secondly, the Vishnu Purana explains that the peculiarly difficult conditions of the Kali Yuga are compensated for. It tells the story of how the great sage Vyasa, while taking his ritual bath in the Ganges, was one day heard to exclaim, 'Excellent, excellent is the Kali age'. The Brahmins who overheard him could hardly believe their ears, and afterwards they hurried to him for an explanation. Vyasa explained to them that he spoke as he did because in the Kali age account is taken of the state into which men have fallen, and of the difficult conditions that prevail. As a result, a small act of virtue performed in the Kali Yuga has the same effect as a great and difficult act of penance would do in an earlier age. Both the Hindu devotional movement and the Tantric tradition take their cue from this, claiming that their methods are 'easy' or 'natural' and especially adapted to the conditions of the Kali Yuga.

The Six Schools of Philosophy

The stages of the process by which the universe emanates from the Supreme Reality are set out in the philosophy of the Sankhya school. Its concepts, probably formulated early in the first millennium B.C., have come to permeate the whole of Hindu thought. In particular, the ideas of the Sankhya school were grafted onto the ancient Yoga tradition of India, and it is this marriage which provided the basis for the Yoga school of Patanjali. However, in the Yoga school the emphasis is changed, and interest centres not on broad universal theory, but on individual salvation and the techniques which can bring this about. Before we turn to these two schools, it will be helpful to understand their place within the broader pattern of Hindu thought.

The Sankhya and Yoga schools belong to the six *darshanas* or 'views' of Hinduism. These are the six main schools of philosophy which, since they acknowledge the authority of the Vedas, fall within the Hindu framework. There has in the past been vigorous debate between these six *darshanas*; yet they can also be viewed as complementary – six different stages of a single process, seeking the same objective, *moksha* or release. The six schools fall conveniently into pairs:

1. Sankhya and Yoga. These two schools hold many views in common, except that the outlook of Yoga is theistic while Sankhya has no God. Yoga is primarily concerned with the nature of man and with practical method; Sankhya supplies the broader macrocosmic picture, and regards knowledge alone as sufficient for release. Although the Sankhya is no longer an active school, its ideas are of great importance as they have passed into the general current of Hindu thought. In these two schools, and especially Yoga, some of the oldest indigenous ideas of India may have found a home.

2. Mimamsa and Vedanta. These two schools relate directly to the Vedas. The older school, the Mimamsa (a word meaning 'enquiry'), inherits the Vedic tradition of the Brahmins, and it arose in an attempt to check the decline of interest in the old sacrificial religion. For it, Dharma, in the sense of living according to the religious rules and performing the prescribed rituals, is all-important. It places the emphasis on the earlier parts of the Vedas, in particular the Brahmanas, and is conservative in nature. The Vedanta, which is also called the Uttara Mimamsa ('the later or final enquiry'), emphasizes the Upanishads as the true source of metaphysical knowledge. It interprets the rest of the Vedas in their light, being concerned to draw out the implications of the Upanishadic sayings, and to present them in terms of a coherent system. Whereas the Mimamsa school has long ceased to be active, the Vedanta has come to dominate Hinduism intellectually.

3. The Nyaya and Vaisheshika schools are of less interest in the present context. The former is concerned with the processes by which we know, and methods of logical analysis. The latter is primarily interested in the physical world and the categories of existence. It is to a large extent an early form of physical science.

The Sankhya World-View

In the Buddhist literature we are told how the future Buddha was directed at the start of his search to two well-regarded teachers dwelling in a forest. From the description of the doctrines they offered the Buddha, they seem to have been early representatives of the Sankhya or Yoga schools. If the Buddhist report is true, these traditions must have been emerging in the same period of religious ferment which also gave birth to the Upanishads and to Buddhism itself.

Although the Sankhya school is no longer an active force it remains important. Many of its ideas have been borrowed by later systems, notably the Vedanta. As the first systematic account, it has provided the basic 'map of the universe' for Hindu thought. In speaking of the Hindu view of the world one is speaking very largely of the Sankhya view.

The word Sankhya means 'numbering', and the Sankhya philosophy is an attempt to enumerate and understand the stages by which the different elements which make up the universe come into being. It is concerned, not with the celestial world of the gods and their relation to man, but with the world as we experience it. It is a way of knowledge, an attempt to win liberation by grasping the nature of the universe and of man as a part of that universe.

Purusha and Prakriti

The Sankhya starts from two fundamental realities called *Purusha* and *Prakriti*. What human beings experience is, on the one hand, multiple points of consciousness, that is to say living beings (including oneself); and on the other hand, a world of inanimate matter. Sankhya calls these two principles Purusha, the principle of consciousness and animation, and Prakriti, primal matter or substance. Beyond these it does not seek to enquire: for the Sankhya, Purusha and Prakriti already lie on the very frontier of human thought, and whatever unifying cause may (or may not) lie beyond them is not available to knowledge. The Sankhya philosophy therefore has the appearance of a dualistic system.

Prakriti is an important concept in Hindu thought. It is said to be inert, indestructible, all-pervasive, and eternal. It is not matter as we know it, but something more fundamental than this. Matter as we know it is always conditioned and differentiated by form – by qualities of one sort or another. Prakriti is matter as it is prior to this conditioning. It is formless matter (the 'Prime Matter' of Aristotle); pure potential; the original substance of the universe out of which all things come and to which they return. Since Prakriti has no form there is nothing to differentiate it. Two consequences follow from this. First, Prakriti is one. And second, it cannot be perceived or known.

Atman

Purusha is the complementary principle. The word Purusha is found in the Rig Veda; and in the Upanishads it is used almost synonymously with the term Atman. But the Sankhya understanding is different. For the Sankhya school, Purusha is multiple: there are as many *purushas* as there are beings in the universe. Although they are separate, they are said to be identical in nature. Like Prakriti, the *purushas* are eternal and never cease to be.

Purusha and Prakriti, then, are opposite principles, quite different in nature and forming a radical duality. Neither one can act without the other. Purusha on its own has no substance, and consequently no vehicle of expression. Prakriti by itself is inanimate and can do nothing; it must remain potential only. Yet it is from the coming together of Purusha and Prakriti that all things arise. Manifestation *is* their interaction.

The Unrolling of the Universe

Somehow, and the Sankhya does not attempt to explain how, Purusha and Prakriti come into contact or 'association' (*samyoga*). This initiates the process of *shrishti*, literally the 'unrolling' of the universe. It is not a creation because everything already exists in potential in Prakriti. The forms appear, but in reality nothing new

47

has been created. Just as a foetus starts to form in the womb as a result of contact with the male principle, the potential for manifestation lying within Prakriti begins to stir upon contact with Purusha.

The process which follows is described by the Sankhya in terms of *tattvas*. These are a series of twenty-five principles, or steps in the emanation of the universe. The first two *tattvas* are Purusha and Prakriti. The third *tattva*, the initial result of their contact, is simply called Mahat or Maha-tattva, 'the Great Principle'. This is sometimes translated as Cosmic Ideation, and is perhaps comparable to the Christian concept of the Logos. It is the loss of the state of perfect balance in which Prakriti had rested prior to manifestation: the first stage of differentiation, from which everything else will come forth.

When viewed in relation to man, this third *tattva* is called Buddhi. Buddhi is the highest faculty in man. Like everything else in the world it consists of Prakriti, even though it is matter in an extremely subtle form. In this subtle matter, in itself inert, the *purusha* is reflected, just as the sun is reflected in a pool of water. In this way, for the first time, consciousness becomes confused with matter, as the *purusha* erroneously identifies with Buddhi. The initial step towards individualized existence, and the arising of the empirical world which is its counterpart, has been taken. Buddhi, then, is the earliest phase in the limitation of consciousness: the possibility, but not as yet the actuality, of being a subject.

The fourth *tattva* is Ahamkara, which is the actualization of that possibility. The word means 'I-maker', and it is the principle of individuation, the emergence of the idea of the individual 'I'. From this point on the subject-object distinction upon which our experience of the world rests comes progressively into being. There follow Manas, the mind (the fifth *tattva*), and as its agents the five powers of perception (the powers to hear, feel, see, taste, smell) and the five powers of action (speech, movement, grasping, procreation, excretion). Finally there arise the elements of the physical universe (the last ten *tattvas*): first the five subtle elements (called *tanmatras*) which, it is held, lie behind and give rise to the material elements; and finally the material elements themselves: *akasha* ('the invisible'), i.e. space, often translated as 'ether', air (or the principle of movement), fire (or the principle of luminosity), water (or the principle of liquidity and flexibility), and earth (or the principle of solidity and stability).

This then is the Sankhya view – and to a large extent the Hindu view – of the coming into being of the world. For the Sankhya school (but not for some later schools such as Advaita Vedanta) the whole of this process is real: Purusha is real, Prakriti is real, and the empirical world which results from their interaction is also real.

The Three Gunas

Another important aspect of the Sankhya teaching which has passed into the mainstream of Hindu thought is the idea of the three Gunas. This word is derived from a root meaning to twist, and the Gunas are conceived as the three strands which, twisted together, make up a rope. That rope is Prakriti, the cosmic substance. Prakriti *is* the Gunas, and consists of nothing other than them.

The three Gunas are modes of being, tendencies of existence, and in varying combinations they pervade everything that is. *Rajas* is the principle of activity, *tamas* that which restrains and obstructs, and *sattva* that of harmony and clarity. When Prakriti is in its undisturbed state before the emanation of the universe these three Gunas lie within it in perfect balance. They embrace each other in a primordial unity, but they have not ceased to exist. On contact with Purusha the balance between them is disturbed; it is this disturbance which sets in train the chain reaction which takes the form of the *tattvas*. The altered balance produces a new form, in which one or other of the Gunas predominates. This new form then reacts separately with all three of the Gunas, producing further forms; and these again interact both with each other and with the three original Gunas. In this way an infinite variety of combinations arises, and this is the manifested universe.

Finally, the Gunas are never found separately or in their absolutely pure forms. All three are present in everything and in everyone, but always in different proportions and combinations. Nothing which partakes of Prakriti is devoid of the three Gunas. Both the outer physical world and the inner mental world are their expression. We may think we act, but in reality it is not *purusha* which acts; it is the Gunas of Prakriti which act through us.

Release in the Sankhya

The Sankhya philosophy differs from the Yoga school in that it finds no place for a personal God. Consequently there is no idea of grace; release is won purely by knowledge. Our real being is the *purusha*, the unchanging spirit present in each one of us. This has become confused with Prakriti. We are caught within the processes of the material world, like a bird entangled in the net of the Gunas. We feel ourselves constricted, caged – 'fastened to a dying animal', in the phrase of W.B. Yeats. The means of release, according to the Sankhya, is to understand this situation, and by means of careful discrimination and meditation to free the *purusha* that we really are from its entanglement with Prakriti. Then for us rebirth will terminate.

The Yoga Tradition

Holding broadly the same view of the world-process as the Sankhya is that aspect of Hindu tradition which is perhaps most widely known in the West, Yoga. The word Yoga conveys the idea of joining or bringing together, and Yoga may be interpreted both in the sense of a method – that of self-discipline – and of an objective, the reintegration of the *jiva* with the Atman. Yoga is not so much a philosophy as a tradition of practice, perhaps one of the oldest such traditions known to the world. Its approach and techniques are found in Jainism and Buddhism, as well as pervading much of the Hindu tradition.

As an old and flourishing tradition, Yoga has developed many branches and sub-schools; among its well-known forms are Hatha Yoga, Kriya Yoga, Laya Yoga, Shabda Yoga, Raja Yoga. We find Atma Yoga and Adhyatma Yoga mentioned in the Upanishads;[2] and in one of the later Upanishads a sixfold Yoga is described in some detail, and an old verse quoted:

> *The oneness of the breath and mind,*
> *And likewise of the senses,*
> *And the relinquishment of all conditions*
> *   of existence –*
> *This is designated as Yoga.*[3]

Yoga is a prominent theme in the Bhagavad Gita,[4] where the word is used to mean the way of practice, as opposed to Sankhya, the way of knowledge. Indeed, the pervasiveness of the idea of Yoga is shown by the use of the terms Bhakti Yoga, Jnana Yoga and Karma Yoga – general designations for broad Hindu approaches rather than specific techniques.

The objective of Yoga, like that of the Sankhya, is to free the *purushas* from painful entanglement with Prakriti, but it differs from the Sankhya in holding that knowledge alone is not sufficient to effect this: 'Perfection in Yoga is not achieved by mere reading of the scriptures', as one text tells us.[5] Even with a perfect theoretical knowledge of the distinction of the *purushas* from Prakriti, man, in the view of the Yoga school, remains entangled, and this is because of the nature of his mind and the manner in which it is conditioned by Karma. The problem is deep-seated: we have identified with the mind and the individual self which it serves for many incarnations.

The Eightfold Yoga

The ancient Yoga tradition took on the characteristics of one of the six *darshanas* or 'views' of Hinduism when the Yoga Sutra of Patanjali was composed, probably in the third century A.D. Patanjali defines Yoga as *citta-vritti-nirodha*, 'suppression of the fluctuations of the mind', and he sets out eight stages of the process by which this is brought about.[6]

The first two stages (*yama* and *niyama*) are concerned with the moral life. Controlling this and bringing it into a state of order is the essential precondition for all further progress, for without it the mind can never be restrained. Such virtues as non-injury (*ahimsa*) of other creatures, truthfulness, purity, contentedness and self-study are necessary. Next come posture (*asana*), control of the breath and energy flows (*pranayama*), and withdrawal of the senses (*pratya-hara*). These are not merely physical practices, but stages in the withdrawal of the mind from the physical world which stimulates it and supplies it with its objects. Of posture Patanjali says only that it should be firm and comfortable. The objective is mental concentra-tion, and the many elaborate and difficult postures and exercises developed later by the Hatha Yoga school do not form part of his system. What is much more central is *pranayama*, control of the *prana*. *Prana* is usually translated as 'breath', but it is really much more than this. It is not just the air in our lungs, but the flow of psycho-physical energy which derives from this and, coursing through the living being, finds expression in the activity of the mind and in desires, emotions and actions: 'When there is movement of *prana* in the appropriate channels, then there is movement in consciousness and mind arises.'[7] In consequence of this, to the extent that the breathing can be brought under conscious control, so too can the activity of the mind. In particular, the systematic lengthening of the pauses between inhalation and exhalation slow down and can even temporarily arrest the mind. Since *prana* is the life-energy, manipulating it in these and other ways has definite dangers, and it must only be attempted under competent supervision. It is the *prana* which withdraws from the body at death, and taking with it the other subtle elements migrates to a new body.

From the control of the mind, the fifth stage, the withdrawal of the senses from their objects, follows; for it is the mind which directs the senses. This stage is well described in a verse of the Bhagavad Gita:

> *And when, like a tortoise withdrawing its limbs*
> *on all sides, he withdraws the senses from their*
> *objects, his wisdom is steadied.*[8]

The Way to Samadhi

Once the mind is isolated in this way and no longer fed with the stimulation flowing to it through the senses, the last three stages can be undertaken. The three steps which follow describe the final

53

stages in the arresting of the mind, and the disentangling of the pure consciousness or *purusha* from Prakriti. These are concentration (*dharana*), meditation (*dhyana*), and absorption (*samadhi*). In concentration the mind becomes 'one-pointed' and is brought to bear on a particular object of thought, and in *dhyana* it is stabilized in this in a powerful and uninterrupted flow.

The final stage has two levels. In the first, '*samadhi* with cognition' (*samprajnata samadhi*), the awareness of distinction between subject and object has vanished. All movements of the mind have been eliminated and there is awareness only of the object of meditation. *Samadhi* in this sense is not in fact rare. It occurs, however briefly, every time we are utterly absorbed in something for itself alone, and entirely without reference to any self-interest – deep contemplation of a work of art or of natural beauty, for example. For the moment all our attention is concentrated on the object and we cease to be aware of ourself as the subject. The individual self with its never-ending worries and concerns is forgotten, and with the disappearance of the ego we experience a moment of deep happiness. That is *samprajnata samadhi*, although in the normal way our experience of it is so brief, fragmentary and undisciplined that we are hardly aware of it. Under the discipline of Yoga it is sustained, guided and controlled.

In the final level, '*samadhi* with no cognition' (*asamprajnata samadhi*), even the last trace of the presence of Prakriti in the form of the object of contemplation vanishes. The awareness of the object as well as that of the subject has now gone. Since we can only think in subject-object terms we cannot know what this means. We can only experience it for ourselves. The mind which for so long stood between us and our true nature has been overcome, and what is left is pure consciousness devoid of any object. With the disappearance of the mind, the seeds of rebirth which it contains and which lie deep within it are burnt up. The goal of the 'restraint of the fluctuations of the mind' has been reached. The *purusha* is freed from the effects of Prakriti and ceaselessly experiences the bliss of its own nature.

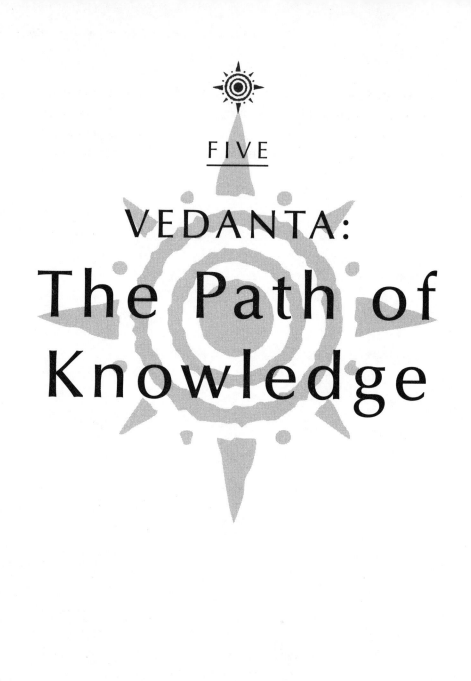

FIVE

VEDANTA: The Path of Knowledge

After the Sankhya-Yoga tradition, we come to the second important strand woven together with the Vedic core in the formation of Hinduism. This is the Vedanta. The Vedanta is called *jnana-marga*, 'the path of knowledge', and in terms of ideas it is the most influential element of all. Its name proclaims its dependence on the Vedas. *Vedanta* means 'end of the Veda', and the term can be read either as a reference to the importance this school attaches to the last part of the Vedas, the Upanishads; or as a claim to represent the complete knowledge of the Vedas, to be their culmination.

There are different schools of thought within the Vedanta, but the term is most often used with reference to the earliest of these. This is the Advaita or 'Non-Dual' Vedanta, given its classical form by one of the greatest of India's thinkers, Shankara. No doctrine has influenced Hindu thought more than this, and all other schools of Vedanta have had to take account of Shankara's position. In this chapter we shall be concerned only with this school; the more important of the later schools relate to the Bhakti or devotional movement.

The foundation text of the Vedanta school is the Brahma Sutra (also called the Vedanta Sutra). It is not known when these verses were composed (guesses range between 200 B.C. and 400 A.D.), but they are so brief and compressed as to be almost incomprehensible without the aid of a commentary; in fact, their importance lies in the famous commentaries by Shankara, Ramanuja and others they have inspired. These short, cryptic verses – memory triggers for those who already knew the teachings – are the tip of an iceberg, the surviving evidence of a continuous tradition going back in all probability to the Upanishads themselves. The Brahma Sutra mentions some of the earlier teachers, but we know nothing more than their names. We do, however, know the central figure of the Vedanta school. This

is Shankara, whose brief but amazingly productive life probably ended about 725 A.D.

Shankara

Shankara is one of the great figures in the history of Indian thought. It has been said of his main work, the famous commentary on the Brahma Sutra, that it is 'the single most influential philosophical text in India today', standing 'at the pinnacle of Indian philosophical compositions'.[1] This work, together with his commentaries on the principle Upanishads and the Bhagavad Gita, won for Advaita Vedanta its central role in Hindu philosophy. Later thinkers who wished to challenge Shankara's views felt obliged to do so by composing commentaries upon the same texts, which came to be recognized as the 'three foundations' (*Prasthana-traya*) of the Vedanta. In the West, Shankara has long been recognized as among the world's greatest philosophers.

In spite of his fame, we know little that is certain about his life. The traditional accounts, which date from a much later period, tell us he was born into a Brahmin family in what is now the state of Kerala in the far south of India. Abandoning his Brahmin status along with everything else at the age of nineteen, he became a *sannyasin*, a wandering monk. His pupil, Sureshvara, describes him as 'a lordly ascetic who walked with a single bamboo staff', and as 'a noble-minded man who had swept away all the impurities from his heart'.[2] He travelled to northern India and there won renown at Benares and other centres in the great public debates on scriptural interpretation which were an important feature of Indian life. It is said that many pupils, themselves spiritually advanced, flocked to him. He travelled widely and established four famous monasteries which still exist in the North, South, East and West of India. He died at thirty-two, from a snakebite according to some accounts, leaving behind him not only his writings but one of the great monastic orders of Hinduism, that known as the *Dashanamis* ('ten names').

Shankara's Philosophy

The Vedanta is not interested in cosmology or the processes of creation. All such schemes are for it symbolic and mythical, and in these areas it is content to borrow from the Sankhya and Yoga traditions. What interests the thinkers of the Vedanta is the reality-status of the world, and the real nature of oneself: the question, *Who am I?*, takes on a central importance. 'The noble ones,' writes Shankara, 'the seekers of liberation, are preoccupied only with the ultimate reality, not with useless speculations about creation. Hence the various alternative theories about creation come only from believers in the doctrine that creation is real.'[3]

It is a widely accepted principle of Indian thought that anything which changes cannot, in an ultimate and final sense, be real. Reality is not something which comes and goes. It requires stability of being; as the Bhagavad Gita puts it: 'For the unreal there is no being, nor any end of being for the real.'[4] This constitutes a difference with Western habits of thought. In the West, reality is generally equated with experience coming to us through the senses. It is, first and foremost, the material world – hard, solid, objective, 'out there', independent of us. This view goes back at least to Aristotle and, although modern physics has made some inroads into it, it remains dominant. It is not at all the view of Shankara. For him, the material world – the world of growth and decay, of never-ending flux and change – is precisely what is *not* real.

All that has form is subject to change. It has some stability of being, and therefore a provisional reality, but sooner or later it changes and in doing so reveals its unreal nature. And if the whole universe is subject to change, this only means that reality itself, final and absolute Reality, must lie in some other order of being. This is why Shankara's philosophy is called Advaita or 'Non-Dual' Vedanta. The meaning is that absolute reality lies in a different order of being, outside the duality of the subject-object mode of knowing. That mode of knowing normally prescribes the whole of our experience; it is characteristic of the individual self and of its principal instrument, the mind. Shankara's message, therefore, is a radical one: the world around us *and* the human individual which experiences it are both of them ultimately unreal.

Shankara is concerned with removing the ignorance of our own nature which keeps us bound to the phenomenal world; with clearing away the self-imposed obstacles which stand between us and an immediate apprehension of our own innermost reality. These ideas are present in the Upanishads; but the Upanishads, although they contain piercing insights, record the thoughts of many different sages and follow no particular order. The objective of the Vedanta is to derive from them a systematic philosophy. For this school of thought, it is not so much more faith in gods which is required, but more scepticism about the reality of the world and of the individual self which experiences it.

Degrees of Reality

The basis of Shankara's method was to distinguish between different degrees or levels of reality. There can of course be only one reality as such, and it is as we have seen that which never changes its nature. The Upanishads call it Brahman. And in man it is Atman, the unchanging consciousness which lights up the changing forms of experience. In the *Panchadashi*, a celebrated Advaita treatise written some six hundred years after Shankara, the Atman is likened to the light which illumines a theatre:

> *There is a witness-consciousness in the jiva which*
> *reveals at one and the same time the agent, the*
> *action, and the mutually distinct external objects.*
> *The witness persists through all the mental*
> *experiences of hearing, touching, seeing, tasting*
> *and smelling, just as a light illumines everything*
> *in a theatre. The light in the theatre reveals*
> *impartially the master of the house, the guests*
> *and the dancer. When she and the others are*
> *absent, the light continues to shine forth*
> *revealing their absence . . . In this illustration the*
> *master of the house is the ego (ahamkara), the*
> *various sense-objects are the guests, the intellect*
> *(i.e. the mind) is the dancer, the musicians playing*
> *on their instruments are the sense-organs, and*
> *the light illuminating them all is the witness-*
> *consciousness. The light reveals all the objects in*
> *the theatre but does not itself move. So the*
> *witness-consciousness, itself motionless, illumines*
> *the objects within and without (i.e. the internal*
> *world of subjective experience and the 'objective'*
> *world of external experience).*[5]

This inner light which witnesses the flow of the appearances making up experience is the unchanging reality, without which nothing else would be. Yet each appearance while it lasts has a temporary and provisional reality for those enclosed within its bounds. In this way, consciousness in its individualized forms experiences at different times different levels of reality, each of which seems absolute while it lasts. While we are dreaming, the world of the dream and our experiences in it are quite real for us. It is only when we wake up that this changes. What happens then is that our consciousness moves onto another plane of reality, one that is more stable and therefore closer to absolute reality. In relation to this new level, the lower level – that of the dream – is now seen to have been unreal. But waking life too exists at a certain level. Once again, while we are enclosed within it, its reality seems to us total, but one day – when we die, or when we attain release – we will find that it too was only a greater and more stable kind of dream.

Thus there are different levels of reality: the purely subjective reality of dreams and day-dreams; the more stable reality of the apparently objective world; and perhaps above that other levels which are more stable still, and which the Vedas call 'the world of the gods' or 'the heaven of Indra'. Ultimately *all* such experiences are found to be unreal and only absolute reality, Brahman-Atman, the canvas upon which they have been painted, truly *is*; awareness of this being the state of *moksha*, release from illusory 'realities'.

The True Self and the Apparent Self

We have already encountered the roots of the idea of different orders of reality. They lie far back in the Rig Vedic verse, taken up and repeated in the Upanishads, which speaks of 'Two Birds' seated in the same tree. Similarly the Aitareya Upanishad asks, 'What is it that we worship as this Self? Which of the two is the Self?'[6] Shankara comments on this, 'we are aware of two entities within the body, an instrument which assumes various different forms and *through which* we have empirical knowledge, and a single (changeless) principle which *has* knowledge'.[7]

These two entities, Atman and *jiva*, correspond to different levels of being: Atman to absolute reality (hence its identity with Brahman) and *jiva* to all the levels of partial and provisional reality which the individual self experiences. To each the world appears in a different light. From the viewpoint of the Atman, the ever-unattached witness-Self, neither the world of phenomena nor the individual self which experiences it have any final reality whatsoever. This is the ultimate and unqualified truth. To one who has attained to this state – that is, who is *jivan-mukta* ('released while living') – the empirical world, whilst it continues to appear so long as he remains in the body, is seen and known as a dream: it ceases to be an object separate from the subject. Gaudapada, Shankara's predecessor in the Advaita tradition, speaks of 'experts in the Upanishadic wisdom who look upon the world as if it were a cloud-city seen in a dream'.[8] But from the viewpoint of the individual self, the *jiva*, the world is perfectly real. The *jiva* is not wrong in taking the world to be real. For the *jiva*, it is real. The individual self and the empirical world which it experiences are complementary; the two halves of a single phenomenon, as real as each other. Without the world – or anyway, *a* world – to experience there is and there can be no individual self. If we ask, 'Is the world an illusion?', we must answer 'Yes' from the absolute point of view, but 'No' from our present point of view which is that of the *jiva*.

Saguna and Nirguna Brahman

Just as there is a real Self and an illusory self, so there are two ways of viewing the ultimate reality, Brahman. We have seen that Brahman in its own nature is ineffable and can only be defined negatively, in terms such as the 'not this, not this' of the Upanishads. This is Nirguna Brahman – 'Brahman without qualities'; Brahman seen from the standpoint of ultimate truth, and entirely apart from the Gunas or qualities.

But Brahman may also be seen from the relative standpoint, the standpoint of the *jiva*. In this context He appears as Ishvara, the 'Lord' of the universe, superior to the individual soul and separate from it; and then He not only has qualities, but is the source of all qualities. This is Saguna Brahman – 'Brahman with qualities'; Brahman as He is known in terms of attributes; Brahman as the human mind can conceive Him.

These are not of course two different Brahmans, but two different ways of understanding the same Brahman. Saguna Brahman is the personal God of religion who occupies a central place in the devotional tradition within Hinduism. Shankara gives this point of view full recognition in his commentary on the Bhagavad Gita. Nevertheless, for Shankara it remains an understanding which is valid at the level of provisional reality only, for it is only at that level that any forms whatsoever can appear.

Thus it is the mind, with its need to conceive objects and qualities which it can grasp, which separates us from the Absolute Reality. It is our individuality itself that keeps us from our own real nature. Any position whatsoever which depends upon the mind and its forms *must* fall short of ultimate reality. Any form capable of conceptualization, and therefore dependent upon the mind, cannot be the final truth. All those schools which fail to step outside the forms of the mind must preclude themselves from the ultimate truth. For this reason a famous Advaita text, the *Yoga Vasishtha*, comments: 'For those who have not known the essential nature of the Deity, the worship of form and the like has been prescribed. To one who is incapable of travelling a distance of one Yojana (8 miles), a distance of one Krosha (2 miles) is provided.'[9]

From the viewpoint of Advaita, an ultimate reality which is personal is a contradiction in terms, a 'conditioned Unconditioned'. However valuable such an idea may be at the level of provisional reality and practical religion, it cannot be the final truth. Shankara writes:

> *When one becomes awake to the non-difference of the individual soul and the Absolute through such texts . . . as 'That thou art', this puts an end to the notion that the individual soul is suffering transmigration and also to the notion that the Absolute is a World-Creator. For all empirical notions of distinction, which are introduced by error, are cancelled and eradicated by right knowledge.*[10]

Maya

Brahman and the world of phenomena, Atman and the individual self or *jiva* – these are, Shankara says, opposites, two different orders of reality. The reality in which the individual self lives and the mind operates has as its form duality, the subject-object mode of being. Brahman and Atman – two words which refer to one and the same reality – are of another order of being: they are *Advaita*, Non-Dual. From the dual viewpoint – that of a subject which experiences objects – the Non-Dual offers nothing to grasp and so appears as void. But once we step across the line, and instead of identifying with the individual soul identify with the Atman behind it, the situation is reversed. Then we see in a Non-Dual fashion. What at present seems unreal is then experienced as the Real, and what now seems real is seen to be illusory.

There is no link between different orders of reality, and this disjunction is what the Vedanta calls *Maya* – the word means 'illusion' or 'magic'. Maya is simply a name for something which can never be explained. It is the hiatus between two different realms of being; the interface between Reality as such and the provisional and apparent reality which the individual self experiences and exists in.

This is why life is so mysterious to us, why thought and speech turn back baffled from Brahman, and why certain questions can never be answered. Answers are only possible in terms of the world the mind inhabits. When we ask, *When did the universe begin?*, or, *Why did the universe come into being?*, we are already assuming the existence of time and of causality. But time, space and causality are *part* of the universe – they are its basis – and they have no existence or application outside it. Questions as to the origin of the universe – that is to say, of manifestation as a whole – can never be answered, but we *can* understand why they cannot be answered. It is because the question itself assumes the existence of the universe (i.e. of time, space, and causality), while at the same time asking about its origin. It therefore has no meaning. Our minds can only function within the framework of time, space and causality; that is, within the phenomenal universe. Maya is the name for what happens when we reach its frontier.

Superimposition

For Shankara the error from which all others arise is that we do not distinguish the degrees of reality. We superimpose the attributes of the relative level (i.e. of the *jiva*) upon absolute reality (the Atman), and vice versa. This is Avidya, ignorance, the root cause of all our troubles. We continually confuse our nature as the unchanging witness (Atman) with our ultimately fictitious nature as an individual (*jiva*) in the world of appearances. Shankara's term for this confusion is *adhyasa*, superimposition. In the opening sentence of his commentary on the Brahma Sutra, Shankara explains that the two, unchanging witness or subject-consciousness and all that is object for it (the empirical world, including our individual self), are of opposite natures 'like darkness and light'. They exist on different planes of being. And yet, he continues, it is for man a natural procedure (natural because it is precisely this procedure which makes man what he is, so that the procedure is coextensive with man) to fail to distinguish the two, and to superimpose upon each the nature of the other. In this way we confuse the truly real with the ultimately un-real. States and activities of the body-mind are attributed to the Self, the pure centre of consciousness. We say, 'I am stout, lean, fair, standing, walking, jumping'. Or, vice-versa: the Self is superimposed on the body-mind complex, and we say, 'it hurts me', when in fact it hurts the body; 'I am tired', when the limbs or the mind are tired.

Rope and Snake

To illustrate this Shankara uses the example of a man who is walking along a path at twilight. He sees something lying in the dust just in front of him. It is a snake. A tremor of fear runs through him. Quickly he looks for something to defend himself with. But suddenly he sees that it is not a snake at all, but just a piece of old rope lying there quite harmlessly. He relaxes, laughs at his mistake, and goes on his way. This is superimposition (*adhyasa*). The characteristics of one thing (the snake) have been superimposed upon something else which is in reality quite different, and on this basis the man has become involved in emotions and actions.

We should notice, however, that the illusion rests on something real, the rope. It is because the rope is there, but is not clearly known, that the superimposition takes place. In the same way the individual mind and the world it perceives are superimposed on a reality which has not been properly grasped, the Atman. It is the imperfectly perceived Reality lying behind them which gives to the empirical world and the individual self their seeming and provisional reality.

Thus we, who are in our true nature pure blissful consciousness, unchanging and unattached to anything whatsoever, the precondition and ground of all appearance, identify with the mind, the emotions, the body, our family, our nation, our house, our car, and all the rest of it. In a word, we limit consciousness, we become the *jiva*, the individual, subject to Karma and full of needs and wants and worries. The individual self is not a reality: it is an *upadhi*, a 'limiting adjunct' placed upon the Atman and obscuring its reality. The cause of this fall is wrong knowledge. Its cure is correct knowledge, *jnana*.

In short, we have forgotten who we are, and the process leading to enlightenment is the process of rediscovering – not just in theory, of course, but as living experience – our own real nature. Enlightenment is the correction of an error, a change in self-identity. It occurs at the moment when we no longer identify with the limited individual self (which continues to appear but has ceased to be important to us), but with the unchanging beam of consciousness which stands behind it and illumines all experience. This is why the Mundaka Upanishad can declare:

> *He, verily, who knows that supreme Brahman,*
> *becomes Brahman.*[11]

SIX

THE NATURE
of Man:
Rebirth and
Karma

For Vedanta it is knowledge which brings release, and this view has become widely diffused within Hinduism. But it should not be thought that the Vedanta is simply a theoretical and intellectual enterprise: 'You should contemplate this truth again and again, and reflect upon it from beginning to end. You should march along this path now . . . If you conceptualize this teaching for your intellectual entertainment and do not let it act in your life, you will stumble and fall like a blind man.'[1] The theory is important, but it is not enough. It must be turned into living knowledge.

This is done by a programme which gradually reduces identity with the individual self: by disciplining the senses and the appetites without resorting to extreme asceticism, loving kindness to others, surrender to the Guru, harmlessness to other creatures, gentle and considerate speech, meditation on texts affirming one's identity with Brahman, the repetition of brief verbal formulae (*mantras*), visualization practices in which the Self is contemplated under symbolic forms, and perhaps by breathing exercises borrowed from the Yoga school. Association with others similarly engaged, and the personal guidance of a Guru who has himself traversed the path, are important. By these means the inner faculties are purified, and the individuality becomes increasingly transparent. At last a real change in being starts to occur: the identity begins to shift away from the individual self to the Atman, which up until then has been concealed behind the *jiva*, like the sun behind a cloud.

Anything less than this change of identity will not be sufficient, for the ultimate truth about the human condition is not something which can be grasped by the individual self or by the mind which is its instrument. Our minds are themselves deeply implicated in the world-illusion. In the view of the Vedanta, the understanding that the truth lies beyond what can be said, or what the mind can grasp, is the true mysticism.

We have seen that the inner reality of man is not the mind. Nor is it the individual self which the mind serves and expresses. It is the Atman, the unchanging consciousness which stands behind and illumines all else. Consciousness may be likened to pure light; the mind to a window made of different coloured glasses which conditions it. The whole purpose is to remove the conditioning, and to know and identify with the Atman in its purity. That is release.

In Western thought, mind or intelligence is not distinguished from consciousness. The two are taken as the same, intelligence simply being regarded as the highest expression of consciousness. It is quite different in India. Here, a clear distinction is made between consciousness and the intellect or mind: 'the fundamental difference between Western and Eastern psychology is that the former *does not*, and the latter *does* differentiate Mind from Consciousness'.[2] Mind is not the same as consciousness; on the contrary, it is that which limits and conditions it. From the Hindu point of view, the failure of Western thought to distinguish between mind and consciousness is a fundamental error, and an important source of weakness.[3]

This difference affects the whole understanding of man. Whereas Western thought, particularly since Descartes, makes the fundamental distinction within man that between mind and body, Hindu thought places it quite differently. For Hinduism, the important difference is that between consciousness on the one hand, and the mind-body complex on the other. The two, as we have seen, belong to different orders of reality. The mind is not distinct from the phenomenal world, but exists within it and as part of it. It is physical in nature, composed of a subtle form of Prakriti, and therefore not essentially different from the body. Hinduism, like Buddhism, is deeply concerned with the nature of man, with the different functions and attributes of the individuality. Psychology was not invented in the West. There is a long tradition in the East in which the make-up of man and the manner in which he is conditioned is explored.

The Make-up of Man

In the Katha Upanishad there is a well-known passage in which the human being is likened to a chariot.[4] Plato, too, used this analogy, and the same imagery occurs at the start of the Bhagavad Gita.

In the Katha Upanishad passage the chariot is the human body; the chariot-driver is the highest faculty of the individual self, the Buddhi; the reins he uses, and which must at all times be held firmly in his hands, are the Manas or lower mind; the horses, which may be well-trained or unruly, are the senses; and the ground they range over are all the objects which the senses encounter. In this chariot rides the Self, the Atman – but when it becomes identified with the mind and senses, the Upanishad tells us, it is then 'the enjoyer'. These, then, are some of the elements in the make-up of man. We have already encountered several of the terms in the Sankhya philosophy, but let us now examine them in this new context.

First, riding in the chariot we have the Self. But when the Self is superimposed upon the mind and confused with it, it seems to be 'the enjoyer', the bird who tastes the fruit, the individual self or *jiva*. Steering this self on its journey and controlling the whole apparatus in which it travels through life is the charioteer, the Buddhi. The Buddhi is not easy to define. It is the closest of our faculties to the

Atman – that 'higher' aspect of the mind which guides one's life. It does not argue and weigh the pros and cons, but it grasps knowledge and meaning, discriminates and judges, selects and resolves. The word Buddhi is often translated as 'intellect', and it does correspond to that broader and higher concept of Reason which once prevailed in the West. But the Buddhi also has about it something of the Western idea of the conscience. In its true nature it is the faculty of dispassionate and therefore true judgement, the source of wisdom, idealism, and prudence. It knows what is right. But it can also be swayed by emotions and become corrupted by self-interest.

The instrument through which the Buddhi operates is Manas, the lower mind. There are two sides to Manas. In one aspect it is the sense-mind, and it is often regarded in Indian thought as the sixth of the senses; the hub from which the other five senses (as well as the five powers of action) radiate outwards. Through it the self makes contact with external objects, whether these appear in dream or waking. It recognizes and interprets the impressions which the five senses send back to it, building them into perceptions and giving shape to the external world.

But Manas is also discursive thought. It debates and doubts, compares, calculates outcomes. It does not make decisions, but places possibilities before the Buddhi. Whereas the Buddhi is in principle dispassionate and impartial, Manas is entirely driven by desires and fears. During waking life and dream it never rests, placing a continual stream of impressions, impulses, likes and dislikes, desires and emotions before the Buddhi. The taut, vibrating reins of Manas link the Buddhi to the senses, and draw the *jiva* out into the world of phenomena.

To these elements we must add several more not mentioned in the analogy. Chief of these is *Ahamkara*. We saw in an earlier chapter that this is the 'I-maker', the principle of individuation, our awareness of ourself as a distinct individual with his or her own interests to protect. In the hierarchy of the elements making up the inner world of man, Ahamkara is placed below Buddhi and above Manas. Buddhi is in principle supra-individual, the faculty which knows things as they are. So long as its place in the hierarchy is maintained, its judgements are uninfluenced by self-interest. But when the personality falls into confusion, then the Buddhi may come under the sway of Ahamkara and will no longer be able to perform its function of judgement correctly. Manas on the other hand is situated below Ahamkara, and is in consequence entirely concerned with personal interests. It looks at everything in terms of these. That is its nature, and self-reference is never absent from its calculations.

The last important element in the make-up of man is *Citta* (not to be confused with *Cit*, which means consciousness). The word comes from a root meaning 'to accumulate'. Sometimes Citta is used simply to denote the mind as a whole, but in its more specialized aspect it is that part of the mind in which memories accumulate; both conscious memories, and, far more importantly, the deep-seated, unconscious, emotional memories which condition the individual. Citta is above all the subconscious mind, and we shall see that it is the seat of Karma.

Om – *The Primordial Sound*

There is another manner in which the inner being of man, and indeed of totality itself, is represented. This is by means of the symbol, or rather the sound, *Om*. *Om* is thought of as the primordial

Figure 4. Om – the Primordial Sound

sound from which the entire universe came forth. It is held by Hindus to be Brahman itself in the form of sound:

> *All Vedanta, nay, all the philosophy of the Hindus*
> *is simply an exposition of this syllable* Om. Om
> *covers the whole universe. There is not a law, not*
> *a force in the whole world, not an object in all the*
> *world which is not comprised by the syllable* Om.
> *One by one you will see that all the planes of*
> *being, all the worlds, all phases of existence are*
> *covered by this syllable.*[5]

When written in the script of India the sound *Om* has four parts. The three curves which are joined together stand for the three levels of

75

reality within which the individualized consciousness of man moves. The lowest curve is the world of waking experience, corresponding to the physical body and to the material universe. The middle curve is the dreaming state of man and corresponds to the mental life; the inner world of dreams, imagination, and subjective experience. The curve above this is said to represent the state of dreamless sleep, during which in Shankara's opinion consciousness persists (for when we awake we are aware that we have slept soundly). It corresponds to what is called the *karana sharira* or 'causal body': the ground, said to be 'subtler than the subtlest', from which the other two states arise. This is the root of manifestation, and the seed of the very existence of the *jiva*.

Above these three curves is a dot, which has an arc below it to emphasize its separation from the rest. This dot stands for that other order of reality which lies altogether outside manifestation, and can never be grasped by the mind. It is simply called *Turiya*, 'the Fourth'. In Shankara's words, 'It is the pure Self, beyond word and meaning, beyond speech and mind. It represents the final dissolution of the universe, the blissful non-dual principle.'[6]

Thus, to meditate on the symbol *Om* is to meditate upon the different levels of being as these occur in our existence, and again as they are reflected in the universe at large. Shankara explains that by means of concentration the individual self is to be gathered together and then precipitated into the *Turiya*, the transcendent Reality, united with it as an arrow is shot into a target:

> *Take up the great bow found in the Upanishads.*
> *Fix in it an arrow sharpened by constant*
> *meditation, which means 'trained'. Then draw the*
> *bow. That is, withdraw the mind and senses from*

*their natural objects and concentrate them on the
one target or goal . . .* Om *is the bow.* Om *is the
instrument that enables the arrow of the
empirical self to pierce the Imperishable Principle,
as the bow is the instrument that enables an
arrow to pierce its target.*[7]

Rebirth

The belief that the individual soul, the *jiva*, is born again into this
world in another body is not part of the oldest Vedic tradition, and
it may be that this is an idea which belonged to the indigenous
peoples of India. In any case, it is present in the earliest of the
Upanishads. Here we are told that, just as a leech or a caterpillar
which has reached the end of a blade of grass, draws itself together
and then stretches forward to a new blade, the individual soul, on
the approach of death, gathers up its powers and then, departing
the body, reaches out towards a new one.[8] Even the gods, according
to some accounts, form part of the chain of rebirths, which extends
from the lowest to the highest beings.

Hindus are not agreed as to what form a future life may take. One
view is that it is by no means certain that one will be reborn in the
human state; animal rebirth is quite possible. Human life is hard to
obtain; it is a rare privilege reached only after many animal incarnations, and the unique opportunity of enlightenment it offers is on
no account to be wasted. Another view, which perhaps has better
backing, is that once a *jiva*, after many previous incarnations, has
attained the human state a threshold has been reached. He or she
will not slip back into an animal form, unless under the most excep-
tional circumstances, and possibly not even then. But, important as

77

such questions may seem, they are in a sense details; the central point is that in the Hindu view rebirth, in one form or another, will take place.

Karma

The cause of rebirth may be summarized in a single word – Karma. Karma is not in itself a difficult concept; indeed, it is the logical outcome of what has gone before. We have seen that the belief in an inherent order in the universe – expressed by the idea of *rita* in the Vedic period, and of *dharma* in later times – has deep roots in the Hindu tradition. If we combine this with rebirth, the natural outcome is the concept of Karma. Karma is no more than the idea of causality applied to the moral sphere. Most people accept that nothing in the physical realm happens without a cause; Hindus merely extend this principle to the moral sphere. Again, we accept that there is at least some linkage between a person's thoughts and actions, and the kind of life he or she experiences. Hinduism, in the doctrine of Karma, simply applies this principle consistently. Our Karma is the outcome of our own past merit and demerit. Causality is as all-pervasive in the moral sphere as it is in the material one.

Every action we carry out, every experience we undergo, in so far as it impacts upon the emotions, leaves a trace in the mind. The stronger the emotion, the deeper the mark that it leaves. In the Hindu psychology, these unconscious mental impressions are called *vasanas*, and in time they build up into deep-seated patterns, etched into the being of the *jiva*. An established pattern of this sort is a *samskara*, a deeply rooted unconscious tendency – emotional impulses, likes and dislikes, hopes and fears – conditioning the individual self. The *samskaras* limit our freedom of action. They determine our character; to a considerable extent, they *are* the individual self. While the conscious memory does not survive death, these patterns, hidden far down within the Citta – the emotional memory – carry over from one life to another. In a manner we do not understand, they determine the circumstances of rebirth. In this way every child enters (or rather, re-enters) the world already conditioned by the *samskaras* of earlier lives. Lying for the moment dormant within the Citta, they will to a large extent determine his or her future life.

Thus Karma, which is nothing but the *samskaras*, is not something imposed from outside. It is the manner in which we have made ourselves: 'Coarse and fine, many in number, the embodied one chooses forms according to his own qualities.'[9] Nor is it correct to see in Karma a doctrine of absolute determinism. While to a large extent our situation is determined by the *samskaras*, there is always some freedom of choice within the limits they impose. How we use that freedom determines our future situation, modifying the *samskaras*, and increasing or decreasing our future freedom of action.

The real problem which the process of Karma poses for the individual is not that it gives us no choice, but that it is self-perpetuating, giving rise to an endless cycle of lives and deaths. One life generates the conditions for the next. At each death the unresolved urges, the *samskaras* lying deep in the inner being of man, draw the *jiva* back into the world. This is the circle of life and death, the unending wheel of rebirth upon which the individual revolves. Shankara summarizes the situation as follows:

> *I am other than the body . . . I am the one who,*
> *from the force of the merit and demerit of my*
> *past actions, entered into the body like a bird*

79

*entering into a nest. And on the death of the
present body I again and again proceed to other
bodies through the force of merit and demerit,
as a bird proceeds to other nests after the first
one has been destroyed. Similarly, in this
beginningless cycle of transmigration, I acquired
and lost many a body through the force of merit
and demerit arising from my deeds, appearing
and disappearing as god, man and beast,
revolving helplessly on the wheel of birth and
death like a bucket fixed to a machine at a well.
Eventually I arrived at my present body . . .
Bodies come and go like clothes.*[10]

This then is the situation of the individual self or *jiva*. Release or *moksha* is release from Karma, from the conditioning of the *samskaras*. And the various 'paths' of Hinduism are so many ways of modifying the *samskaras*: preventing the formation of new ones (Karma Yoga), replacing negative *samskaras* with others which are spiritually more fruitful (Bhakti Yoga), and even of undercutting the entire process by grasping its merely apparent nature and essential unreality (Jnana Yoga).

SEVEN

THE BHAKTI
Movement

After the Yoga and Vedanta traditions we come to the third important element contributing to Hinduism, the Bhakti movement. In terms of popular religion it must be accorded the first place, for it is without doubt the most widespread and visible expression of Hinduism.

The word *Bhakti* means devotion. The aspects of Hinduism we have examined so far have been centred on knowledge. The old sacrificial religion of the Vedic period was a matter of knowing what was required, and the Brahmins were the custodians of this knowledge. The sages of the Upanishads were also concerned with knowledge – knowledge of ourselves, knowledge of Brahman. Sankhya, too, was a way of knowledge; and even the Yoga school, for all its emphasis on practical technique, is based on knowledge. From all of these the Bhakti movement differs. It is a recognition of the importance of the emotional life. Man is not just intellect. He is also emotion and will, heart and feeling. These are the forces which give him energy and direct his actions and thought. They are the wellsprings of his life.

The Bhakti movement believes that man wants to love the good, and that if this is placed before him he will be drawn to it. It seeks not to by-pass the emotions but to integrate them into the spiritual life, to utilize them in the interests of spiritual growth; as a result it has been able to offer an effective religious path to the broad masses of men and women in India. Bhakti sets no preconditions. It requires no learning. It is open to all.

The Bhakti movement is broad and many-sided, and we can only touch on some of its aspects. It is first seen as a distinct form around the fourth century B.C., when several groups appear who worshipped a supreme God under such names as Vasudeva Bhagavan ('the

Adorable One'), Narayana, and Hari. In time, all of these came to be identified with the Vedic god, Vishnu. Also identified with Vishnu were two notable figures appearing in the epic literature, Krishna and Rama: both were seen as his *avataras* or incarnations. In consequence, Vishnu grew greatly in stature and became for millions of Hindus not just one god among others, but the supreme God: God himself.

Others focused in a similar way upon the god Shiva. We have seen that some aspects of Shiva probably go back to the Indus Valley civilization; others belonged to the Vedic god, Rudra, with whom he merged. From then on, Vishnu and Shiva, each regarded by his adherents as God himself, have been the principle recipients of the great flood of devotion which is the Bhakti movement. Nevertheless, Bhakti tends to be associated more closely with Vishnu than it is with Shiva. This is because the cult of Vishnu is almost entirely encompassed by the Bhakti movement; while in the worship of Shiva, devotion is only one of several important elements – for example, Shiva is also thought of as the Great Yogi. Hence, Bhakti and Vaishnavism are terms which are often, if somewhat inaccurately, used as synonyms.

The Bhagavad Gita

We have left to a late point what is probably the best known work in the literature of Hinduism. The Bhagavad Gita – 'the Song of Bhagavan, the Adorable One' – is the first great monument of the Bhakti movement. Although it does not form part of the Vedas, it is greatly esteemed by almost all Hindus.

The Gita is not a separate book, but an episode embedded in a vast epic poem, the Mahabharata. This tells the story of a great war

Figure 5. The god Shiva

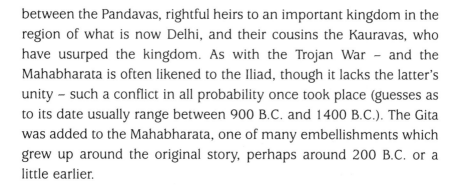

between the Pandavas, rightful heirs to an important kingdom in the region of what is now Delhi, and their cousins the Kauravas, who have usurped the kingdom. As with the Trojan War – and the Mahabharata is often likened to the Iliad, though it lacks the latter's unity – such a conflict in all probability once took place (guesses as to its date usually range between 900 B.C. and 1400 B.C.). The Gita was added to the Mahabharata, one of many embellishments which grew up around the original story, perhaps around 200 B.C. or a little earlier.

The Gita has the form of a dialogue between Arjuna, the leading warrior among the Pandavas, and his friend, Krishna, the prince of Dvaraka, who is acting as his charioteer. It is dramatically placed at the climax of the epic tale. The two mighty armies are drawn up face to face, and in a short while the final battle will be joined. As the first arrows begin to fall, Arjuna and Krishna range in their chariot between the armies and stop to view the opposing force. Arjuna looks on those he is to fight, and is suddenly assailed by doubt. It is not fear which troubles him, for no warrior is more courageous or skilful than he. It is doubt about the morality of what he is about to do. The slaughter will be fearful. There in the opposing army he sees men he grew up with, close kinsmen, loved and revered teachers. All these he must strive to kill. Surely, nothing could justify that terrible act? It would be better to be slain oneself without resistance, he cries out, than to commit the sin of slaughtering one's own relatives. The great Arjuna sinks to the floor of his chariot, his heart shaken with indecision and grief. It is Krishna's reply which forms the rest of the dialogue; and, perhaps surprisingly, he tells Arjuna that he should fight.

The setting in which the dialogue takes place is packed with symbolic meanings. The opposing armies represent duality, inseparable from life in the world. The chariot is the same chariot of man that

85

we found in the Katha Upanishad (see p. 72). Arjuna is the *jiva*, the individual soul – brave, active, energetic, yet entrapped and bemused, torn between the opposing forces of good and evil, right and wrong, pain and pleasure. The only change is that the charioteer, instead of being the Buddhi, the higher mind, is now the Lord himself, the divine reality dwelling in the heart of every being. According to the Indian rules of chivalry, charioteers were not regarded as combatants – Krishna, the Atman, is not himself engaged in the battle of life; he stands apart as its witness. The kinsmen and revered teachers in the opposing army, whom Arjuna shrinks from destroying, are significant: they are those elements in the individuality to which we attach value, but which nevertheless must be sacrificed if we are to come to the supra-individual Self.

The teaching which Arjuna receives is complex, and it ranges across the whole spectrum of Hinduism as it then was. While the Gita is first and foremost a Bhakti work, it is also more than this. Its greatness lies in the way in which it unites the principal tendencies of the time, knitting together the Sankhya and Yoga traditions with the insights of the Upanishads and those of the Bhakti movement. The result, typically Hindu, is a powerful synthesis, in place of fragmentation into opposed positions.

The Gita teaches that there are three Yogas, or disciplines, by which the spiritual end of life may be attained. These are Karma Yoga, Bhakti Yoga, and Jnana Yoga – the ways of action, love, and knowledge – and to some extent they are three stages of a single process. Jnana Yoga, the way of knowledge, we have already encountered, and it is possible to read the Gita as giving it first place. However, the Gita was composed long before the time of Shankara, and in it Jnana Yoga is associated with the ancient Sankhya tradition, as well as with the Upanishadic tradition.

Karma Yoga, the way of action, is the discipline of detached activity, and it forms an important part of the Gita's teaching. It is our emotional engagement in action, not action in itself, which binds us to the wheel of rebirth. Krishna tells Arjuna that the real Self of man does not act, and in the battle to come it will neither kill nor be killed. Our bodies and minds are formed of Prakriti. We think that it is we who act, but in reality it is the three Gunas of Prakriti which do so.

The Gunas move ceaselessly in all phenomena, and whilst we are in the body they will never cease to act in us. It is no good trying to withdraw from action, as Arjuna proposes: for an embodied being, action can never be avoided. What matters is that we should not identify with action – that we should maintain awareness of our changeless inner identity, standing apart from all activity. Actions bind when we lose this identity and believe that it is we ourselves in our full reality who act. Then there is emotional involvement. Then the *vasanas* are formed. Then we are bound by our self-created Karma.

Since there is no escaping action, the only question is what sort of action we undertake. If we act from personal motives, there is the creation of Karma. Therefore, Krishna says, it is what is ordained by duty, or *dharma*, which is to be done. The wise man acts as duty and necessity dictate; and in Arjuna's case, he will perform his *dharma* as a warrior upon the battlefield. Such a man acts without attachment. He does not seek the fruit of action. He accepts whatever comes with equanimity, knowing that in their innermost reality men and women are untouched by all that happens. This is the art of living – Karma Yoga, the Yoga of action.

But of the three paths, that which receives most emphasis in the Gita is Bhakti Yoga, devotion to the Lord. Krishna himself is this Lord. He is Bhagavan, the Adorable One. For those who follow the way of devotion, the Supreme Reality is not unknowable. The Supreme Reality is *Ishvara*, 'the Lord', personal, loving, merciful, and responsive to our love. He is everywhere, the whole universe is His body. As the Upanishads recognized, He is not only beyond qualities (Nirguna) but also with qualities (Saguna), not only transcendent but also immanent:

> *Thou art the dark blue butterfly, and the green*
> *parrot with red eyes. Thou art the thunder-cloud,*
> *the seasons and the oceans. Thou art without*
> *beginning, and beyond all time and space. Thou*
> *art He from whom all the worlds are born.*[1]

Vishnu, the Supreme Reality, is the inexhaustible treasure-house of the universe, from which all its forms, all its beauty and glory, come forth. Halfway through the Bhagavad Gita, Krishna reveals to Arjuna, son of Pandu, His universal form as the Supreme Lord, the infinitely glorious Being who is the source of all:

> *Such as would be the radiance of a thousand suns*
> *bursting forth suddenly in the sky, such was the*
> *radiance of that Mighty Spirit. There the son of*
> *Pandu beheld the whole world with all its*
> *differences, gathered together in the body of*
> *that God of gods.*[2]

But this vision of Totality is not, for the individual self, a comforting one. It is, the Gita tells us, both wonderful and terrible, and before it the worlds tremble. Even Arjuna can barely sustain it. He sees the great warriors of both armies crushed by the relentless passage of time, and all the forms of the universe flowing towards destruction. Yet the mighty Lord of the Universe, within whose being those forms exist and pass away, is at the same time close to us. He is in the chariot of Arjuna, the Lord dwelling in the heart of every creature. At the end of the Bhagavad Gita, Krishna tells Arjuna:

> *Hear further My ultimate word, most secret of*
> *all; thou art exceeding dear to Me, therefore will*
> *I speak what is good for thee. Set thy heart on*
> *Me, full of love for Me, sacrificing to Me, make*
> *obeisance to Me, and thou shalt come to Me; this*
> *is truth I promise thee, for thou art dear to Me.*
> *Putting aside all other duties, come for refuge to*
> *Me alone; grieve not, for I shall set thee free*
> *from all sins.*[3]

'Come for refuge to Me' – that is the essential message of Bhakti.

Bhakti in South India

Throughout the first millenium A.D. the Bhakti movement grew in strength. The South of India played an important part in this; so much so that some sources claim that Bhakti is a product of the South. Between the seventh and ninth centuries, the devotional movement attained a level of very great intensity in the Tamil-speaking areas of South India.

Here, two groups of poet-saints, the sixty-three Nayanars or 'Leaders' who were devotees of Shiva, and the twelve Alvars who worshipped Vishnu and his *avatara* Krishna, exerted a profound influence which continues to this day. The Alvars and Nayanars claim no merit for themselves. They throw themselves upon the mercy of Vishnu or of Shiva. For them, self-surrender is the way to salvation. One worships not by means of sacrifice or meditation, but by devotion and service, given without thought of return. One is saved not through one's own efforts, but by the Lord's grace. Constant remembrance of God and calling upon His name will attract that grace. Rather than seeking to transcend the individual condition in the manner of the Vedanta, they seek an intense relationship with God which implies a separate existence of the individual. They seek to enjoy His presence after death, and in life to experience His divine beauty spread throughout the world:

> *Blessed, blessed is the world; the dark curse on*
> *life is lifted.*
> *Wasting has been laid waste, and hell is in ruins.*
> *Worn-out Death has nothing he can call his here.*
> *Behold, the dark ages are dead,*
> *For everywhere on the earth myriads of*
> *God's servitors*
> *Are singing and dancing, dancing and singing*
> *His praise.*[4]

The Nayanars and Alvars established a pattern which later came to characterize the Bhakti movement right across India. First, since the individual's relationship with God was all-important, they tended to disregard traditional religious forms and the restrictions of the caste system. In consequence, the Bhakti movement took on at times an almost revolutionary character, so that initially it was sometimes opposed by the Brahmins. High caste and low caste, rich and poor, men and women, learned and ignorant, all could follow this path. Nammalvar, the greatest of the Alvar poets, of whose songs it was said that they contained the essence of the Four Vedas, was a lowly Shudra; Kulashekhar was a king; Andal, another of the Alvar saints and one of the most famous poets of India, was a low-caste woman. The independent spirit of these two groups is seen in one of the Nayanar songs:

> *We are not subject to any; we are not afraid*
>   *of death;*
> *We will not suffer in hell; we live in no illusion;*
> *We feel elated; we know no ills; we bend to none;*
> *It is all one happiness for us . . .*[5]

Secondly, they expressed their vision by means of songs which were composed, not in the usual language of literature and religion, Sanskrit, but in the vernacular – in their case, the Tamil language. This was in keeping with the popular character of the Bhakti movement. They wrote in a manner with which everyone could identify. Their religious insights are expressed in the language of familiar human feeling, often that of passionate love:

> *He has kissed these shoulders, these breasts;*
> *And I know not where to turn for refuge.*
> *I am the flower*
> *That the Divine Bee has sucked and torn.*[6]

These songs, combining deep religious feeling with poetic merit and musical beauty, spread rapidly among the people. They have never been forgotten. To this day, they are known and loved throughout the Tamil lands.

The Puranas

A very different expression of the Bhakti movement, which developed around the same time, was the Puranic literature. The word *purana* means 'ancient', and the Puranas recorded old traditions which had accumulated outside the Vedas. Under the influence of the various sects of the Bhakti movement, they were largely recast and revised, while entire new Puranas were added.

There are eighteen major Puranas. They act as a storehouse for the traditional lore of Hinduism, recounting old ideas about the origin of the world and tales of the gods and sages; at the same time, they adapt them to give first place to their favoured deity – usually Vishnu, Shiva, or the goddess, Devi. Recited before large audiences, the Puranas, rather than the Vedas, became the real scriptures of the devotional movement.

In the Puranas we see a different and a much more orthodox face of the Bhakti movement than that presented by the Alvars, or by some of the later singer-saints of North India. The Puranas were composed in Sanskrit by Brahmins, and they combine commitment to the devotional movement with support for orthodoxy. As the Bhakti movement expanded, increasing numbers of Brahmins went over to it. Having lost much of the strength deriving from the old Vedic religion, they were now able to draw upon the surging new energies of the devotional movement. With it, the Brahmins gained a new lease of life, fashioning a synthesis between their own traditions and the new ideas. In the end, most of the leading figures in the new developments came to be drawn from their ranks. Brahmins founded temples, or even entire *sampradayas* or sects, and these remained associated with their descendants. At the present time, the great Bhakti sects are among the principal strongholds of the Brahmins.

Ramanuja

The two traditions, that of the Alvars and that of the Brahmins who had embraced the Bhakti movement, came together during the eleventh century in the person of Ramanuja. Ramanuja was a Brahmin from the Tamil country, who attached the highest value to the songs of the Alvars. He was also deeply learned in the Sanskrit tradition, so that he was able to argue for Bhakti positions in terms acceptable to learned circles throughout India. In this way he provided the theoretical basis upon which a large part of the Bhakti movement, not just in the South but throughout India, was to rest in future.

Ramanuja set out to construct a new model of the Vedanta, a different interpretation of the three texts on which Shankara had based his position – the Upanishads, the Brahma Sutra, and the Bhagavad Gita. He had two objectives: first, to demonstrate the orthodoxy of Vaishnava devotionalism; and, second, to show the superiority of devotion as a way of salvation. Subsequently, other Vaishnava teachers were to follow his example and propound still other versions of the Vedanta, each designed to support a particular devotional school. Each later system moved further away from the Upanishads and closer to the Puranas as its authority.

These efforts of Ramanuja and the later Vaishnava teachers have been influential, but the usefulness of their attempts to give the Bhakti movement an independent theoretical base is doubtful. The essence of Bhakti is that it is not theoretical. It is a way of practice, not a way of knowledge; and in it theory is always, in the end, made subservient to the practical requirements of the path. The real achievements of the Bhakti schools do not lie in the realm of theory, but in that of practice.

94   *Figure 6. The Lord Rama*

The Later Bhakti Movement

During the last thousand years the Bhakti movement, particularly in its Vaishnava forms, has continued to flourish. The great Shri *sampradaya*, named after Vishnu's consort, the goddess Shri, is closely associated with Ramanuja. It is today the oldest of the Bhakti sects, and a pillar of strength in South India. Other traditions are centred on the major incarnations of Vishnu – Rama and Krishna. The story of the Lord Rama, which has spread from India throughout South-East Asia, is told in one of the two great epic poems of India, the Ramayana. The beautiful re-telling of this story in the Hindi language, composed by the poet Tulsidas in the sixteenth century, is today perhaps the most loved and popular book in North India.

At least as widespread and significant is the stream of devotion directed to Krishna, which, as we shall see, has developed in new directions. There is also an important form of the Bhakti movement directed to the formless and unknowable aspect of the Supreme Reality. This is known as Nirguna Bhakti, devotion to the unqualified Brahman, which is sometimes symbolized by, or seen in, the person of the Guru. This form of Bhakti has sometimes been able to find common ground with Muslim spirituality.

Krishna Gopala – The Cowherd Krishna

Early in the sixteenth century, two of the most remarkable and charismatic of the Bhakti teachers, Vallabha (yet another of South Indian stock), and Chaitanya (a Bengali, regarded by his followers as an incarnation of Krishna himself), came to the region of North

India, near the city of Mathura, in which Krishna is believed to have spent his childhood and youth. Here they founded new sects which carried the Bhakti movement to fresh heights of enthusiasm. The Hare Krishna movement, well known in the West, is an authentic branch of the tradition established by Chaitanya.

This new wave of devotion to Krishna centred on a different vision of him from that of the Bhagavad Gita. We have seen that in the Gita, Krishna is a noble and princely figure, standing, as does Rama, for the inner divinity of man at the centre of the great drama of life. But the Bhagavad Gita represents a relatively early stage in the Bhakti movement, and some centuries later (around the third or fourth century A.D.) a seemingly quite different tradition of Krishna emerges – that of Krishna Gopala, 'the Cowherd Krishna'. The magnificence and high drama of the epic literature is set aside and in its place we find a simple, rustic world. The setting now is the land of Braj, near the city of Mathura. Here is the enchanting forest of Vrindavan, through which the great river Yamuna winds on its way to join the Ganges.

Krishna is now found as a mischievous yet delightful child, growing up among the honest cow-herding folk who inhabit the villages of Braj. He takes the cows out to pasture in the forest with the other boys; steals butter, which he greatly loves, whenever he gets a chance; and occasionally, just to remind us that he is an *avatara*, deals with a troublesome demon. Or Krishna is seen a few years later as the youthful and delightful flute-player: as *Murali-manohar*, 'the handsome one with a flute', he is often depicted standing beneath a sacred *kadamba* tree, with his flute to his lips, his legs crossed in a graceful pose, a garland of flowers round his neck. Sometimes a milk-white cow at his side affectionately licks his foot.

Figure 7. Krishna Gopala

All of the Gopis, the beautiful dairy-maids who are the wives and daughters of the herdsmen of Braj, are in love with this handsome and charming Krishna. At the sound of his flute, whether it be night or day, they drop whatever they are doing, leave their husbands and families, and run towards the forest. It was this Krishna, for whom what mattered most was love and who could so easily sweep aside conventions in his pursuit of it, who had inspired much of the devotion of the Alvar poets – Andal, for example, often imagines herself as one of the Gopis. Around the ninth century, the atmosphere of devotion they had created in the South found decisive expression in the Bhagavata Purana, one of the last of the major Puranas, and for devotees of Krishna the most important. In the famous tenth book of this work, the story of Krishna's childhood in the land of Braj and his love for the Gopis is recounted. Full of devotional fervour and charming detail, it has become the classical expression of devotion to Krishna.

From then on the imagery of Krishna's love affair with the Gopis became irresistible. It swept across the whole of India, as poet after poet poured out his or her devotion to Krishna. For a thousand years the arts of Hindu India – poetry and music, drama, painting and dance – have found their greatest inspiration in this vision of love in the blessed land of Braj. The notes of Krishna's flute drifting through the woods are the call of the divine. The butter he loves so much is devotion. The cows he tends are the bounty of nature. The lovely forest of Vrindavan is the world itself, made supremely beautiful by the divine Reality within it.

Thus the objective of Bhakti is fulfilled, and the emotional life of man in all its richness and energy is sublimated and lifted onto the plane of the spiritual life. And, as in all real love, the individual forgets himself or herself utterly and entirely: only the object of love, the divine Krishna, the Lord, the inner Self of man, remains.

EIGHT

THE TANTRIC
Tradition

The last of the four strands which weave together to form the substance of Hinduism is the Tantric tradition. As with the Bhakti movement, Tantrism is not a single, well-defined school, but a broad tendency which takes on many different forms, and its ideas spill over and mix with other traditions. There are Vaishnava forms of Tantrism; Shaivite forms, which are more important; and, as we shall see, Shakta forms in which worship is centred on the Goddess.

While it is certainly Indian in origin, Tantra is confined neither to India nor to Hinduism. It is important in both the Jain religion and in later Buddhism, and in its Buddhist form is found in Central Asia, Tibet, China, Japan, and elsewhere. Whether it is Buddhist or Hindu in origin is uncertain, but its beginnings lie in popular religion and outside the Vedic tradition. Those who teach its practices are not Brahmins, or are Brahmins only incidentally. Like Bhakti it is open to women and all others, without caste restriction.

The tradition takes its name from an important group of texts called *Tantras*. The earliest of these are thought to date to the Gupta Empire in eastern India, around the 4th or 5th century A.D., so that Tantrism emerges as a distinct tradition considerably later than the Bhakti movement. However, elements within it go back to a very much earlier time. One source of its strength lies in the popular religion of India's villages, where the worship of local goddesses is both ancient and widespread. Another important source is in the Yoga tradition, certain aspects of which were taken up and developed by Tantric groups. Philosophically, much has been borrowed from the Sankhya and Advaita Vedanta.

The objective of Tantra does not differ from that of the other major paths of Hinduism; it is release, *moksha* – understood, as in the Yoga and Advaita traditions, as liberation from duality and transcendence of our individual nature. What does distinguish the Tantric tradition is, first, the emphasis it places upon the 'feminine' principle of the universe; and, second, the importance it attributes to practice, *sadhana*, and to the physical body as a vehicle of release. Let us begin with the first of these.

Shakti, The Energy of the Absolute

We saw in the previous chapter that the worship of Vishnu has close links with the Bhakti movement. The Tantric tradition is more closely associated with Shiva, who is often thought of as the un-qualified Absolute or Nirguna Brahman of the Upanishads. As such, he is forever free of qualities, immune from any change or modification. Should Shiva act, he would be subject to change and therefore to limitation. He could then no longer be the ultimate reality. There must therefore be some other power or principle which has brought the universe into being. In Tantric thought, that principle is Shakti.

Shakti means 'energy' or 'power', and Shakti is the energy of Shiva. Through it the One becomes many, and the unconditioned Absolute, unknowable to the human individual, takes on forms. Although in essence the role of Shakti is negative – it limits the Absolute and so produces the forms of the cosmos – from the viewpoint of the world it is supremely positive and creative. For humanity, Shakti is the creative power of Brahman which brings the universe into being, and for this reason is thought of as feminine:

*Before the Beginning of things Thou didst exist
in the form of a Darkness which is beyond both
speech and mind, and of Thee by the creative
desire of the Supreme Brahman was the entire
Universe born.*[1]

Shiva, the Supreme Reality, infinite consciousness, remains ever unchanged, but through his energy or Shakti the ever-changing universe blossoms into being. A verse in one of the Tantric texts puts it succinctly: 'Shiva, when he is united with Shakti, is able to create; otherwise he is unable even to move.'[2]

Although we may separate them in thought, Shiva and Shakti, Awareness and Energy, are the twin aspects of a single principle. They are not distinct, but the complementary poles of one Reality. Shiva, or Brahman, is the immutable basis of all that is; Shakti its moving or active principle: 'If Brahman is the coiled serpent in sleep, Shakti is the same serpent in motion. If Brahman is likened to the word, Shakti is its meaning. If Brahman is like fire, Shakti is its burning power. The two are inseparable: one in two and two in one.'[3]

The Great Goddess

Shakti, the divine source from which all arises, is thought of as the 'wife' of Shiva. She has many mythological forms. Often she is simply Devi, 'the Goddess', or Mahadevi, 'the Great Goddess'. She is also Jagad Mata, 'World Mother'; Ambika, 'Mother'; Uma, who nourishes the world; Parvati, the dutiful wife of Shiva, who seated high in the Himalayas by the side of her Lord represents the stability and continuity of life; the smiling and auspicious Lalita, especially

Figure 8. Parvati, wife of Shiva

worshipped in South India; the ceaselessly warring Durga; and Kali, the destroyer.

It is as Durga that the Goddess is most widely worshipped, and it is she who most fully expresses the energy and complexity of Shakti. Her great festival, Durga Puja or Dussera, lasting for ten days, is an event of great importance. A distinct cult – that of the Shaktas, or worshippers of Shakti – centres on her, and is especially strong in Bengal. For them, the Goddess is the supreme deity, Brahman itself in feminine form. It is the third most popular cult within Hinduism, giving place only to the worship of Vishnu and Shiva in importance.

The name Durga indicates one who is 'hard to approach', and Durga is represented with a stern expression, suitable to the unswerving force which drives the universe. At once supremely beautiful and fierce, Durga rides upon a lion. She may be pictured with four, eight, ten or twenty arms, and in these she brandishes an impressive array of instruments and weapons – conch, discus, trident, bow, arrow, sword, dagger, serpent, mace and other objects. Each has its specific meaning, and taken together they express the ceaseless activity and complexity of Shakti.

Durga is first and foremost a slayer of demons, who are often shown as her victims; they are said to have usurped the role of the gods, and she restores the natural order. She is the goddess of warfare, and in medieval India military campaigns were commenced on the last day of her festival. In Bengal and some other areas blood sacrifices are made to Durga and to Kali, although, as the only blood sacrifices to survive in Hinduism, they are regarded with distaste by the majority of Hindus. Yet at the same time Durga is the all-merciful Mother who nourishes the universe and bestows both material and

Figure 9. The goddess Durga

spiritual wealth. Full of tenderness to those who turn to her, she is greatly beloved by her devotees.

Kali is said to have come forth from the forehead of Durga. If Durga is the fierce side of the Mahadevi, Kali is her terrible aspect: 'She is represented with a black skin, a hideous and terrible countenance, dripping with blood, encircled with snakes, hung round with skulls and human heads, and in all respects resembling a fury rather than a goddess.'4 Rational explanations are offered for the image: her black colour refers to her ultimate nature, which lies beyond mani-festation and is therefore unknowable; the cremation ground on which she is often shown dancing is where all wordly desires are burnt away; the necklace of severed heads is the universe of names and forms which she, as Shiva's power, creates and destroys; she is, as the name Kali suggests, the destructive aspect of time. But the image of Kali, with its pulsating vitality, springs from a more pri-mary level than that of conscious interpretation. It is the recognition of an intuitively grasped truth: Kali is life, seen with all its dangers, bloodshed, suffering, fierce competition and inevitable destruction.

The Ambivalence of Shakti

What the different forms of the Goddess, some smiling and friend-ly, some fierce and terrible, tell us is that Shakti, the energy which shapes and animates existence, is essentially ambivalent. On the one hand, Shakti is the source and sustenance of life, the World-Mother. This is the aspect represented by the auspicious forms of the Goddess; the recognition of the creative and positive aspects of life.

But this is not the whole of Shakti, nor the whole of life. Life also brings with it conflict and suffering, while its end lies in the apparent extinction of death. Nature is not only beautiful and bounteous, but also ruthless and indifferent to the individual. Hinduism does not shy away from this. The images of Durga and Kali are a frank admission of it.

Shakti, like its outcome, life in the world, may be seen in either a negative or a positive light. Viewed negatively, it is the source of all imperfection, ignorance and suffering, the obstacle which stands between us and our transcendent nature. Viewed positively, it is the source of all the joys and benefits of existence, and the context in which spiritual progress can be made. This double aspect is the reflection of our own ambivalence towards the world: we want life, and yet at the same time we long to transcend it.

The Cult of Shakti

The idea of Shakti is fundamental for the Tantric understanding of the world, and it has become an important part of the Hindu outlook. Where the Shakta cult, in some of its manifestations, departs from the Hindu norm, is in forgetting that Shakti is not Reality itself but only the principle which modifies Reality and so gives rise to existence. To worship Shakti in itself is, in the last resort, simply to worship the world and to forget the dimension of transcendence. It can only fasten one more firmly than ever to the wheel of life and death. The greater part of the Tantric movement, especially in its Shaivite forms, does not fall into this error. For it, Shakti is either the complementary principle to that of Shiva; or it is seen as the Supreme Reality itself, but in its transcendent as well as its immanent aspect: 'Indeed thou art neither female, nor male, nor neuter.

WAY of

Thou art inconceivable, immeasurable power, the Being of all which exists, void of all duality, the supreme Brahman, attainable in illumination alone.'[5]

Tantric Practice

If the idea of Shakti is a distinguishing mark of Tantra, it is nevertheless *sadhana*, 'practice', which forms its heart.[6] In the developed Tantric tradition, and in particular in its Shakta forms, there are three classes of aspirants, for each of which a different mode of practice is necessary.

The highest group consists of those who are said to be *divya*, 'godlike'. They are persons in whom the Guna or quality of *sattva* – tranquillity and purity – is dominant. These persons, having passed through the lower stages of Tantric *sadhana*, are far advanced. They, and only they, are fit to undertake the highest stage, that of Kundalini Yoga. The lowest group are those who are *pashu*, 'animal'. In them *tamas-guna*, ignorance and inertia, predominates. For such a person the two higher *sadhanas* are dangerous and unsuitable. He must purify his nature by self-discipline and worship in the normal way.

The middle group consists of those called *vira*, 'heroic', and in them *rajas-guna*, the urge to activity and self-assertion, predominates. They have to overcome their passions and the urge towards gratification of the senses before they can advance to the stage of Kundalini Yoga. The *sadhana* prescribed for this group has caused some Hindus to look with disfavour on Tantra. The practice is called *chakra-puja* or 'circle worship', and is based on the principle, 'By that one must rise, by which one falls'.[7] The aspirants – seated in a circle under the supervision of their Guru – confront under controlled conditions those elements most calculated to excite the passions and (if all goes well!) learn to overcome them. Clearly such a method is open to abuse, but properly executed, it is an exercise in self-control, an attempt to sublimate even the least spiritual aspects of life.

Internalization

The Tantric tradition believes that within man lie all the realities of the cosmos, all its forces, all its deities, right up to the Supreme Brahman. Man is a microcosm of the entire universe, just as, in the earlier Vedic period, the sacrifice was considered to be. But these inner powers lie unrealized within us. We are unaware of them, and experience ourselves only as limited, vulnerable individuals.

The purpose of Tantric *sadhana* is to progressively awaken man's inner being. It must be done in practice. Only by actually experiencing the cosmic realities within ourselves can we become free from our present bondage and realize our identity with Brahman. The means by which this may be done consist chiefly in the internalization of images, and the use of *mantras*.

We have already seen the symbolic character of Hindu images of the gods. In Tantric practice this is put to full use. The image of the deity has to be precisely visualized, and its symbolic content systematically explored. Every detail of the iconography has to be clearly grasped and understood, for it is these which express the powers and qualities of the god. At last the entire image glows within one, every detail alive with profound meaning, and the echoes of the deity within one's own being begin to stir. In this way the image is internalized. Identification with the god becomes possible.

Mantras

Just as the image of a deity, properly evoked, is the reality itself in visual form, so a *mantra* is that same reality in its sound form. We have seen that sound is believed to be the seed and origin of creation, and a *mantra* is the seed or essence of the spiritual reality it evokes. Properly used, it is supremely creative. *Om* is the seed form of Brahman itself from which all things come forth; but every god or goddess has a *bija-mantra* or 'seed-mantra' by which he or she may be evoked. By the use of *mantras*, gods or divine powers can be established in different areas of the body. This practice is called 'placing', and is effected by touching the part of the body concerned while meditating on the god and reciting the appropriate *mantra*.[8]

Kundalini Yoga

The culmination of these ideas, and the supreme *sadhana* of the Tantric tradition, is the practice of Kundalini Yoga. In this the most important *bija-mantras* are 'placed' in six centres of the body, called *chakras* or circles. These *chakras* (which of course exist on the mental, not the material, plane) are visualized as a series of lotuses, occurring one above the other from the base of the spinal column to the centre of the forehead. Each *chakra* is the locus of certain symbols and gods, as well as of a specific *bija-mantra*. Thus the *chakras* represent the cosmic forces lying dormant in man.

At the top of the whole system is the 'thousand-petalled lotus', situated at the crown of the head. This is ultimate reality, Shiva or Brahman itself. The *chakras* are connected to each other and to the thousand-petalled lotus by a subtle channel called the *Sushumna*, which passes through each *chakra* in turn. Two other channels, *ida* and *pingala*, run to the left and right of the *Sushumna* but do not connect with the *chakras*. The energies of man flow through these, and from them circulate to the rest of the body. But in the average man, the central channel, the *Sushumna*, is blocked. The energies do not flow into it, and in consequence they do not reach and awaken the *chakras* and the powers they contain.

At the base of the spine, coiled round the *Sushumna* in the form of a sleeping serpent, is the Kundalini. This 'Serpent Power' is none other than Shakti in its microcosmic form, and it is this which is said to 'block' the *Sushumna*. However, if through intense concentration and Yogic breath-control the sleeping serpent which is Shakti can be awakened, it will cease to block the entrance to the *Sushumna* and will start to rise up this central channel. Then the real energies in man, only the smallest part of which have hitherto been used, at last come into play. As the Kundalini (or Shakti) stirs, it becomes heated with its own awakening energies. It rises up the *Sushumna*, arousing, one after another, the six *chakras*.

As the Kundalini ascends, it draws upwards with it the forces and deities contained in each of the *chakras*, so that the whole awakening inner reality of man rises upwards. At last, and this is the final goal, it reaches the thousand-petalled lotus at the crown of the head, and here the Kundalini and all that it has carried with it is united with the ultimate reality or Brahman. Shakti and Shiva embrace in unity.

In this way, Tantra, by identifying the human body with the spiritual cosmos, seeks to use it symbolically as an instrument by which release from duality may be attained. Rather than engaging in abstract meditation, the Tantric practitioner visualizes the process of liberation as taking place within his or her own body, and this

Figure 10. The Chakras and the three subtle channels

provides a powerful support for what might otherwise seem a difficult and abstract process.

Shakti, or Kundalini, the urge deep within every organism to separate existence, in the ordinary man lies 'asleep' at the opposite pole to Shiva. It blocks the path to spiritual reality. It is 'awoken' – brought into consciousness – and progressively spiritualized. As it becomes one with spiritual reality, the world it creates and the human individuality which goes with it are transcended: 'Shakti reabsorbs the created entities into the unformed state, gathers the seeds of creation, as it were, and brings them back to their primal place of rest. The final union of Shakti with Shiva is, for the person who experiences it, an actual resolution of the duality that constitutes the phenomenal world.'[9]

NINE

THE ROLE OF
the Guru

Wisdom, it has been said by a modern Hindu saint, consists in discovering the real purpose of life and the means to achieve it.[1] The purpose of life, in the view of most Hindu schools, will by now be clear: it is to put an end to our habitual identification with the *jiva*, the transient individual self, and to identify instead with the unchanging consciousness which stands behind it and which alone is Reality.

The four major traditions which we have outlined are different ways to this objective. Although we have treated them separately, they mix and influence one another, and their interplay gives to Hinduism its immense variety and its many subtle nuances. This presents difficulties, as well as advantages, for anyone approaching the Hindu tradition for the first time. Nevertheless, much time and effort can be saved if one understands at least something of the theoretical position. Too often people embark on one or another Hindu practice – a course in Yoga, a meditation class – without any clear idea of its real objective. But meditation and Yoga are most effective when one is clear about what one is trying to do. While they may have incidental advantages to offer, their ultimate purpose is one only: it is *moksha*, release from the individual condition and the wheel of rebirth which goes with it.

Human Birth

According to Hindu tradition the preconditions for *moksha* are three: birth as a human being, the desire to attain release, and the company of spiritually advanced persons.

Birth as a human being is of course the result of one's Karma, and Hindus believe that it represents the fruit of many previous births in animal, and even lower, forms. To live as a human being is a privilege and an opportunity. Only human beings can stand back from the immediate moment and reflect upon their situation, and without this release is not possible. The progress of the *jiva* up through the various levels of animal life to the human condition is a process of emerging individuality. It continues through successive human lives. The individuality becomes sharper as we become more and more conscious of ourselves. But as it does so, we become more aware of the pain suffered both by ourselves and by other beings. Moreover, self-consciousness is intrinsically painful: without knowing it, we constantly flee from the awareness of ourselves as limited, imperfect, vulnerable individuals. Sensual pleasures, entertainment, involvement in work and family – these are all ways in which we seek for a time to escape the nagging consciousness of our own limited nature.

In this way, the development of the individuality reaches a point at which its inherently painful character becomes apparent. The long road outwards, into individual existence and the phenomenal world, has been completed. A turning point has been reached. We sense that we must step into a new dimension which transcends the individual self. This is the point at which we reach the second condition of realization, the desire to attain release.

The Desire for Release

The Hindu believes that we have come into life because we wanted to. That is what Karma really means. Deep-seated longings, in the form of *samskaras*, for experience in the world draw us back. We have only to look at the eagerness with which children and young animals plunge into experience to realize the truth of this. It is no accident, and no decree of an external God or Fate, which determines our birth. It is our own desires. As long as these carry over from one life to another in the form of *samskaras*, we will continue to revolve on the wheel of birth and death. There will be no release.

By means of the Karma Yoga – or action without attachment – described in the Bhagavad Gita, we can influence this process and reduce or even arrest the formation of *samskaras*. Still more effective is Jnana Yoga, the discipline of knowledge. This undercuts the whole process, and, rather than simply inhibiting the formation of future Karma, it can free us from the accumulated Karma of past incarnations. Once the fact that the individual self is ultimately unreal is grasped as a matter of immediate knowledge, then the accumulated store of emotional impulses – the *samskaras* – attaching to that self lose their vitality. They are, it is said, burnt up, like grains of wheat which on being heated lose forever their power to germinate. The methods of the Yoga and Tantric schools have the same purpose, but they seek to achieve it by psycho-physical experience rather than by mental discrimination and contemplation.

A third way of diminishing the individuality and the Karma attaching to it is the way of devotion. This is Bhakti Yoga, a way not of knowledge but of love. This differs somewhat from the other methods. In it the individual self is not regarded as unreal: it is simply set aside, and in its place is put the devotee's chosen deity, or in some schools the Guru. This becomes the new centre of the devotee's world. All the care and concern which was formerly lavished on the individual self is redirected. The individual self is simply forgotten and fades away. For some this is an easier way than the path of knowledge, for it offers not just the denial of the individuality but a powerfully attractive positive ideal in its place.

We have seen that these two ways, the paths of knowledge and devotion, have sometimes been regarded as opposed, or even rival, methods. This, however, is not the most useful approach. In India, the true relationship between Jnana and Bhakti is sometimes illustrated by a story. It tells of a blind man and a lame man, each of whom wants to journey to a certain place. The blind man is the pure *bhakta*. He is strong and energetic and full of enthusiasm. He hurries forward, but he does not see the way; in fact, in his enthusiasm he is in danger of going in the wrong direction or stumbling into the ditch. The lame man is the pure *jnani*. He sees the distant goal, and the entire route stretches out before his eyes. But he makes no progress along the road for his legs do not carry him. His knowledge of the way remains only theory. Thus neither is successful. But if the two can cooperate, and the energy and strength of the one is combined with the discrimination and knowledge of the other, then both can journey successfully to their common goal. In his commentary on the Bhagavad Gita, Shankara speaks of *jnana-nishtha*, 'knowledge-devotion', as the supreme form of Bhakti.[2]

The Guru

The last of the preconditions for release is the company of spiritually advanced persons. This is usually taken to mean association with a Guru and the group of devotees who have gathered round him. The Guru is the link with a particular spiritual tradition. What he teaches came to him from his own Guru, and so on back in a continuous chain. Hindus value tradition for it guarantees a degree of objectivity. The traditional Guru's teaching and his method are tried and tested. They are not his invention; they are not experiments. One of the signs of a genuine Guru is that he makes no claim to originality, but is at pains to emphasize the traditional nature of what he teaches.

The word *Guru* means 'one who dispels darkness', and the word may be applied in different ways.[3] A Guru in India may be simply a family priest: he may have inherited the position; he will have a certain learning, but no special spiritual attainment is implied. Or a Guru may be a teacher who has advanced a certain way along his chosen spiritual path and can guide others over the same ground, without himself having yet attained the final goal. Many teachers in India are in this category, and they may be of real assistance to the spiritual seeker.

Or finally, a Guru may be one who is 'liberated in life', a *jivan-mukta*. While continuing to live in the body, he has discovered – and that is the best word, for the Atman is always present within us – his own innermost reality. Inwardly, he is released for ever from the individual condition, having perceived its relative nature. For him, the world has ceased to exist as something outside his own awareness. Its ultimate unreality is known; but it does not disappear, and others see him still seemingly endowed with a personality and continuing to act in the world:

> *He does all, yet he does nothing. Inwardly having renounced everything, though outwardly he appears to be busy, he is ever in a state of equilibrium. His actions are entirely non-volitional . . . His soft and sweet words are full of wisdom. He has nothing to gain from noble deeds, yet he is noble; he has no longing for pleasure and hence is not tempted by it. He is not attracted to bondage or even to liberation. The net of ignorance and error having been burnt by the fire of wisdom, the bird of his consciousness flies away to liberation.*[4]

This is the ideal or archetypal Guru, the true *jnani* or 'knower', who teaches not on the basis of theoretical knowledge but on that of his own direct experience of spiritual reality. A Guru of this type acts as a lens, concentrating the light and warmth of the spiritual tradition to which he belongs upon those who have gathered round him. His only purpose is service of others. His only desire is to promote spiritual wisdom.

Shri Dada of Aligarh

The Hindu Guru need not be a priest, a monk, or an ascetic, although of course he may be. Two of the outstanding examples of the recent past lived outwardly contrasting lives. Shri Dada of Aligarh (1854–1910) was a married man with several children, who dwelt in the busy towns of northern India where large Muslim communities and the influence of Western technology were a part of life. He worked throughout his life as a junior railway official, in charge of the telegraph office at a succession of stations. He earned little, and what he had was repeatedly given away to those in need. He anticipated Gandhi in his concern for the outcasts of Indian society, and in seeking – sometimes at personal risk – to prevent conflict between Hindus and Muslims. When cholera broke out he spent the nights nursing the poor and disinfecting their homes. But he always placed the spiritual life first; in his view no greater service could be done to anyone than awakening the spiritual life.

Although Shri Dada deliberately sought obscurity, at each town he was transferred to a group of devotees quickly gathered round him. These were people of all classes: simple men and women – a carpenter, a lamplighter – and others who were learned and sophisticated. Shri Dada's outlook was entirely traditional, and he would often attribute his entire spiritual knowledge to his own Guru, claiming nothing for himself. He was always prepared to acknowledge the wisdom and beauties of other religions, and, in line with a long tradition in northern India, would sometimes engage in spiritual discourse with Sufis. His intellectual position was that of Advaita Vedanta, but his methods were often drawn from the Bhakti movement. So closely did he combine the paths of knowledge and of devotion that they became virtually one. He summarized his outlook as follows: 'the highest teaching is *Tat Tvam Asi* ("That Art Thou"). I have found obscurity to be a real friend, simplicity to be the best companion and devotion to my Guru the highest solace in life.'[5]

Shri Ramana Maharishi

The life of Shri Ramana Maharishi (1879–1950) was very different from that of Shri Dada. When a youth of seventeen, he was seized by a profound fear of death. It was in fact an anticipation of the death of the individual self, for what followed was the spontaneous experience of release, attained – most exceptionally – without the assistance of a Guru. He went to Arunachala, a sacred hill in southern India, to live in solitude in a cave. He spent the remainder of his life at Arunachala. As his high spiritual state became known, disciples from both India and the West came to him for guidance. In spite of his contact with others in the role of Guru, Shri Ramana remained inwardly the solitary sage, living a life of great simplicity and ascetic purity. Those who sought his help were guided sometimes by specific teachings, but often only by his silent presence:

> *It was a delightful and unique experience to sit in*
> *the presence of the Maharishi and look at his*
> *beatific eyes. One might go to him with a medley*

*of doubts and questions. But very often it
happened that these upsurgings of the mind died
down and were burnt to ashes as one sat before
the sage.*[6]

Shri Ramana's release came to him without previous theoretical knowledge, yet his insights corresponded to the teaching of Advaita Vedanta. He was 'an incarnation of pure Advaita . . . the eternal impersonal principle in a personal garb'.[7] His instruction to others centred round the question, 'Who is the real "I"?'; to him there was no plurality, and his actions were performed without any sense of attachment.

Shri Ramana insisted that a Guru is a necessity for the spiritual life, yet would never admit in so many words that he himself was any-one's Guru. This, together with the fact that his own release seem-ingly took place without a Guru, caused some to be confused.[8] The explanation lies in Shri Ramana's own spiritual state: to him, the Guru could not be a separate individual existing apart from and out-side the disciple, for all such distinctions were illusory. In his own words: 'The Guru is the formless Self within each one of us. He may appear as a body to guide us, but that is only his disguise.'[9] In fact, the function of the outer Guru is to awaken the inner Guru in the heart: 'Two things are to be done, first to find the Guru outside your-self and then to find the Guru within.'[10]

The Human Situation

No better description of the role of the Guru, and of the human situation as it is understood by Hindus, can be given than that of Shankara. Following the Chandogya Upanishad, he likens the knowledge of the Self to the distant land of Gandhara, the homeland we have lost, and to which we can find our way back with the help and guidance of the compassionate Guru:

> *Consider the case, my dear one, of how in the world some thief might bandage someone's eyes and take him away from the land of the Gandharas and deposit him with his eyes bandaged in some distant spot in the jungle far away from all human life, and how that person, having lost his sense of direction, might yell out at the top of his voice . . . 'I am from Gandhara: my eyes have been bandaged and I have been left here by a thief'. Suppose, then, that some compassionate person freed him from his eye-bandages and said, 'Gandhara is to the north from here. You must first go to such and such a place.' He, being thus freed by the compassionate person from his bandages, would go from village to village, asking the way to the next village each time . . . Such a man would eventually reach Gandhara, though not a person too foolish to understand the instructions, or a person carried away by his desire to see some other place . . .*
>
> *Such also is the case of the one who is torn away from his real condition as the Self of the universe by the merit and demerit arising from former deeds, and deposited in the jungle of the human body . . . He is entangled in the net of a hundred thousand evils in the form of such thoughts as 'I am a man', 'This is my son', 'These are my relatives', 'I am happy', 'I am miserable' . . .*

123

Somehow, through very great merit arising from past deeds, while crying out thus, he manages to find refuge in some supremely compassionate person who has direct knowledge of the fact that his own real Self is pure Being or the Absolute, who is established in the Absolute, and who is free from bondage. From this supremely compassionate person of perfect enlightenment he receives instruction in noting the defects attaching to the objects encountered in transmigratory life. Eventually, when he has become indifferent to the objects of the world, he is taught, 'Thou art not a denizen of the world, with worldly characteristics such as "being the son of so-and-so". Thou art pure Being.' In this way he becomes released from his bandages of nescience and delusion and reaches his own true Self, as the inhabitant of Gandhara reached Gandhara, and becomes happy.[11]

TEN

CONCLUSION

In the course of this short survey we have seen something of the breadth and complexity of the Hindu tradition and the manner in which its forms have shifted. It has been said that Hinduism seems to be a federation of faiths rather than a single religion, and in many ways this is true. Even within a single school, the Vedanta, there are widely different views on such central issues as the nature of Brahman, the status of the individual self, and the reality of the empirical world. Yet there is also much which binds Hinduism together, giving to it an unmistakeable character: belief in rebirth and Karma, the cyclical nature of time, the immanence as well as the transcendence of the Supreme Reality, the less than fully real and ultimately unsatisfactory nature of empirical existence, and the supreme value of *moksha* or release, are among the most widely held ideas.

Moreover, underlying the flexibility and the variety of forms which characterize Hinduism, we can detect a persistent pattern. It is that of a single unchanging Reality – which may be conceived either theistically, or as the unqualified Absolute lying beyond all description – and alongside it, a principle of change and limitation which makes possible all of manifestation. This pattern appears in different guises: as Purusha and Prakriti in the Sankhya and Yoga schools;[1] as Brahman and Avidya (with its outcome, Maya) in Advaita Vedanta; as Vishnu and his 'sport' or *lila* in the greater part of the Bhakti movement; and as Shiva and Shakti in the Tantric tradition. This pair – ultimate reality and principle of manifestation – is the bedrock upon which Hinduism rests; the unchanging metaphysical foundation beneath its varied forms.

While the status of the first of these two principles is quite clear – it is Reality itself – the status of the second (and therefore of the phenomenal world which is its expression) is deeply mysterious.

Indeed, it is the ultimate mystery. The second principle cannot be an independent reality, for Reality can only be one. Some consider it an expression or 'power' of that Reality which is Brahman, a real effect of a real cause – yet how can an unchanging Absolute give rise to an effect? Others see it as having a provisional reality for us, but nevertheless unreal in absolute terms. What is clear is that, whatever degree of reality the second principle possesses, that reality is drawn entirely from its relationship with Brahman. It is not a case of a distinct power of change and manifestation set over and against a transcendent First Principle; to regard it as such would be to misunderstand the whole direction of Hinduism.

Informing the whole of Hinduism is the idea of release or *moksha*. It is essentially a change of identity, a disengagement from the second of the two principles we have discussed and a conscious identification with the first. This is the great goal, the reality and the possibility of which is vouched for by the Upanishadic *rishis*, and by the saints of every generation. *Moksha* is not something which is gained or obtained; it is the discovery of something present in us all the time – a different kind of consciousness which is our ultimate destination simply because it is our innermost nature.

For most schools of Hinduism (though not for the major Bhakti schools), *moksha* is release from the individual condition itself: the release of consciousness from the limiting forms in which it is enclosed, as the relative nature of these is experienced. Thus *moksha* is not a deprivation but an expansion of consciousness beyond the bounds of individuality. It is essentially positive – not, as the Buddhist *nirvana* is often and perhaps incorrectly represented as being, simply the ending of sorrow.

However great the value placed upon *moksha*, the claims of ordinary life are not denied. Hinduism is a religion which is catholic in the full sense of the word, and within it there is room for men and women at every level of development. Just as there are four classes in Hindu society, so too four corresponding objectives in life are recognized. The highest objective is, of course, *moksha*. The other three are: *dharma*, carrying out the obligations and duties stemming from one's social station, as Krishna in the Bhagavad Gita advises Arjuna to do; *artha*, the pursuit by just and fair means of material well-being; and *kama*, the pursuit of love and the pleasures of the flesh in their natural and normal forms.

This breadth and acceptance of life is reinforced by the fact that the Supreme Reality is thought of as immanent in the world, in addition to being transcendent to it. From this comes the great respect which Hindus have for the earth and its gifts – seen, for example, in the love and gratitude felt towards the domestic cow, which is thought of as a living symbol of the bounty of nature. Hinduism is in many respects a joyous religion, as those who have witnessed its festivals will know. While for some who are striving for *moksha* asceticism certainly has its importance, the natural world is not in general seen as opposed to the spiritual life. On the contrary, it is seen as an expression of divinity, and in consequence of this Hinduism recognizes no principle of evil as such. The many demons which inhabit the world of Hindu myth all have their place in the scheme of things, and in the stories they always turn out to be of a spiritual nature and capable of liberation. The life-affirming principle, the power or *shakti* which brings the world into being, is not understood as opposed to the transcendent principle, but is an aspect of it. Shakti is the partner of Shiva, his other face. The serpent which, in Christianity, brought about the Fall of Man and became his lasting enemy, is in Hinduism found entwined around the neck of Shiva, or acting as the couch upon which Vishnu reclines.

But if Hinduism does not deny the world and so slip into dualism, neither does it make the opposite mistake of becoming a mere earth-religion – a faith in which life and nature are celebrated and their benefits sought, while the transcendent dimension is virtually ignored. The natural world is not opposed to the Supreme Reality, but neither is it its entirety, and *moksha* exists on an altogether different plane of being to that of the three other life objectives. It consists, as we have seen, in an entirely different order of consciousness; and in order to discover this, to become what we really are in our deepest being, Hinduism holds that we must free ourselves from all emotional engagement with the world and its forms. That involves, not a denial of the world or the body, not turning against it and seeing it as an enemy, but seeing it in the context of a greater reality, and thus as the relative and temporary thing that it is.

But not everyone will attain to the Self-discovery which is *moksha* in this lifetime. The goal is a possible one, but the hold which life in the world has upon us is powerful and the habit of identity with the individual self deeply engrained; few will attain release, because in reality few of us want it deeply and persistently enough. What, then, will happen to those men and women who, having travelled some part of the way, do not complete the whole journey before death? What has Hinduism to offer these? Are their efforts lost and wasted?

This is a question which will spring to everybody's mind, and it is put to Krishna by Arjuna at the end of the sixth chapter of the Bhagavad Gita. Krishna's reply is that for such a one there is no loss. Although he will inevitably reincarnate, his Karma is such that he will be reborn into spiritually auspicious circumstances, perhaps in a family of persons who are themselves actively seeking release. He will possess the same level of spiritual understanding that he reached in his previous life, and will be able to resume his journey from that base. The momentum of his previous efforts will help to carry him forward, and in this way through different lifetimes he will be able to progress to the highest goal.[2]

In some respects, Hinduism may seem more difficult to approach than other major religious traditions. It is not a missionary religion, in the way that Buddhism or Christianity or Islam are. In the past, believing that people come naturally to whatever path they are suited to, it has not as a rule gone in search of converts. It does not see itself as the only true religion, the only way of salvation, and it does not disturb a Hindu to see that someone else follows another faith.

All of this has meant that Hinduism has remained more closely identified with the land of its birth than have the other major religions. But although its imagery is strongly Indian, there is nothing about its central teachings which limits Hinduism to India. More than a thousand years ago Hinduism spread widely and rapidly in South-East Asia, and during the last one hundred years Indians, aware of a growing need, have made considerable efforts to carry its message to the West – not with the object of converting those who already have a religion, but to offer a path to those who have none. It is not necessary to travel to India to discover Hinduism. There are in most countries in the West genuine groups – as well of course as some which are less genuine, but only the individual can decide on this – attached to one or other of the four major strands of Hindu tradition which have been described in this book.

At a moment of great difficulty in the life of the West, Hinduism, along with the other great religions of the East, offers to Western man a way out of spiritual bankruptcy. The structures, both of Christianity in the West and of the Liberal-Humanist creed which attempted to supplant it, have broken down, and the individual is left to wander in a darkening forest of moral and intellectual chaos. But without a coherent and comprehensive world-view to guide us we cannot avoid serious errors, and life is largely wasted.

In this situation, Hinduism comes before us as an old and authentic path, tested by many centuries of human experience. While recognizing the importance of religious forms, it has not lost sight of their ultimately relative nature. While going far beyond anything that reason can discover for us, its various traditions recognize the claims of reason and are not generally in conflict with it. It offers a vision of man and of his possibilities far different from that to which we have become used: 'Heaven is that which delights the mind; hell is that which gives it pain', the Vishnu Purana tells us.[3] It is a way which demands, not so much acts of faith, but a willingness to listen to the voices of the past, to think clearly about what is important in life, and finally, to make the effort to carry out in one's own life certain practical measures and to observe their result. Hinduism claims to provide systematic means of spiritual progress; methods which are testable. Only by embarking on a particular path and pursuing its methods, can its validity, and its suitability for the individual concerned, be discovered.

WOLVERHAMPTON
PUBLIC LIBRARIES

NOTES AND
Further
Material

Notes and References

Introduction

1. Swami Harshananda, *Hindu Gods and Goddesses*, Mysore, 1981, p. 160.
2. T.M.P. Mahadevan, *Outlines of Hinduism*, Bombay, 1984, pp. 249–50.
3. Shankara's commentary on the Bhagavad Gita; introduction to verse 18.67.
4. In the Shvetashvatara Upanishad (verse 4.2) it is said of Brahman, 'That itself is the fire, That is the sun . . .', and in the very next verse, 'Thou art the woman, Thou art the man . . .'. The implication that the Supreme Reality can be viewed either as Impersonal or as Personal is clear. Swami Tyagisananda, *Shvetashvatara Upanishad*, Madras, 1987, p. 77.
5. Rig Veda, 1.164, verse 46. Griffith's translation.
6. Bhagavad Gita, 2.46.

Chapter One

1. The section which follows describes the view which is still most widely accepted by Western scholarship, resting on the work of the famous nineteenth-century philologist, Max Muller. However, it should be noted that this view is coming more and more under challenge, and that many Indian scholars and an increasing number of Western ones no longer feel able to accept the theory of an Aryan invasion of India. They argue instead that the 'Aryan' or Vedic people were indigenous to the area which is today Pakistan, and that the Indus Valley civilization (see page 5)

was the Vedic civilization. There is considerable evidence for this view, and if it comes to be accepted it will have most important implications, making the Vedic texts very much older than present estimates and altering the entire picture of the early development of civilizations. For a balanced view of the current state of scholarship see B.B. Lal, *New Light on the Indus Civilization*, Aryan Books, New Delhi, 1998, especially pp. 116–123.

2. Rig Veda, 4.38, verses 5–8. Griffith's translation (adapted and abbreviated).

3. F.M. Muller, *India: What Can It Teach Us?*, London, 1883, p. 29.

4. Thomas Hopkins, *The Hindu Religious Tradition*, Belmont, 1971, pp. 4–9.

5. *Ibid.*, pp. 9–10.

6. Rig Veda, 10.90, verses 11–12. Griffith's translation.

7. H.L. Basham, *The Wonder That Was India*, London, 1971, pp. 149–51.

8. This book follows the practice of many authors in using the term *Brahmin* to distinguish the priestly class from the texts, the *Brahmanas*; in Sanskrit the two terms are spelt identically. Both have the meaning 'concerned with *Brahman*', the ultimate Reality. A fourth term, *Brahma* (the masculine form, Brahman being the neuter form), stands for that limited aspect of Brahman responsible for the creation: Brahma is the Creator-God.

9. Some Indian scholars have dated the earliest parts of the Rig Veda as far back as 4000 B.C. See K. Klostermaier, *A Survey of Hinduism*, Albany, 1989, pp. 415–16.

10. The idea emerges at numerous points in Western culture. The Greeks called this principle *physis*. The whole of European classical art rests upon this notion of an

inherent order; so too does the modern ecological movement.

11. The *Purusha Shukta* is Rig Veda, 10.90; the *Gayatri* is found at 3.62, verse 10.

12. Rig Veda, 10.129. Griffith's translation (adapted and abbreviated).

13. See the sections 'The Solar Self' and 'The Sun of Transformation', in D. Frawley, *Wisdom of the Ancient Seers*, Salt Lake City, 1992.

14. K. Klostermaier, op. cit., p. 130.

Chapter Two

1. A.K. Coomaraswamy, 'An Indian Temple', in vol.1 of *Selected Papers* (Ed. R. Lipsey), Princeton, N.J., 1977.

2. Rig Veda, 10.90 (*Purusha Sukta*), verses 6–7. Griffith's translation.

3. Vishnu Purana, 2.14. Wilson's translation.

4. Chandogya Upanishad, 8.12.1. Swami Swahananda's translation.

5. S. Dasgupta, *A History of Indian Philosophy*, vol.1, Delhi, 1975, pp. 30–31.

6. Rig Veda 1,164, verse 6. Hume's translation.

7. Chandogya Upanishad, 3.14, verse 1. Swami Swahananda's translation.

8. Aitareya Upanishad, 3.1, verse 3. Swami Gambhirananda's translation.

9. Chandogya Upanishad, 6.9. Hume's translation.

10. Chandogya Upanishad, 3.1, verse 6. Hume's translation.

11. Kena Upanishad, 1.6 and 1.7. Swami Gambhirananda's translation.

12.   Brihadaranyaka Upanishad, 3.8, verses 8 and 10. Hume's translation.

13.   Rig Veda, 1.164, verse 20. Griffith's translation.

Chapter Three

1.   Vishnu Purana, 1.22. Wilson's translation (slightly adapted).

2.   Alain Danielou, *Hindu Polytheism*, New York, 1985, p. 152.

3.   Danielou, *op. cit.*, p. 155.

4.   Vishnu Purana, 1.22. Wilson's translation.

5.   Karapatri, 'Shri Vishnu Tattva'; cited in Danielou, *op. cit.*, p. 155.

6.   Danielou, *op. cit.*, p. 157.

7.   The author is indebted for much of what follows to two sources: A.K. Coomaraswamy's essay, 'The Dance of Shiva' in the book of the same name (New York, 1924); and H. Zimmer, *Myths and Symbols in Indian Art and Civilisation*, Washington, 1946, pp. 151–6.

8.   Cited by Coomaraswamy, *op. cit.*, p. 60.

Chapter Four

1.   Vishnu Purana, 6.1. Wilson's translation.

2.   M. and J. Stutley, *A Dictionary of Hinduism*, London, 1977, p. 349.

3.   Maitri Upanishad, 6.25. Hume's translation. Cited in Stutley, *op. cit.*, p. 350.

4.   See Bhagavad Gita, 6.11 to 6.29, where the practice of Yoga is described in some detail.

5.   Hathayoga-Pradipika, 1.65; quoted in Georg Feuerstein, *The Yoga-Sutra of Patanjali*, Folkestone, 1979, p. 59.

6. *Yoga-Sutra*, 1.2 and 2.29 ff.

7. *Yoga Vasishtha*, translated by Swami Venkatesananda as *Vasistha's Yoga*, SUNY Press, Albany, 1993, p. 316.

8. Bhagavad Gita, 2.58.

Chapter Five

1. K.H. Potter, *Encyclopedia of Indian Philosophies*, Princeton, N.J., 1977-90: vol.3, *Advaita Vedanta*, pp. 119–20.

2. Cited in A.J. Alston, *A Shankara Source-Book*, vol.1, London, 1980, pp. 44 and 46.

3. Commentary on Gaudapada's *Karikas*, 1.7. Translated by A.J. Alston, *op. cit.*, vol.2 (1980), p. 79.

4. Bhagavad Gita, 2.16.

5. Panchadashi, 10, verses 9–15. Translated by H.P. Shastri, Shanti Sadan, London, 1965.

6. Aitareya Upanishad, 3.1.1. Swami Gambhirananda's translation.

7. Commentary on the Aitareya Upanishad, 3.1.1. Translated by A.J. Alston, *op. cit.*, vol.3 (1981), p. 47.

8. *Karikas* 2.31. Cited in Alston, *op. cit.*, vol.1, p. 27.

9. *The Essence of Yogavasishtha* (translated by Samvid), Samata Books, Madras, 1985, p. 229.

10. Commentary on the Brahma Sutra, 2.1.22. Translated by A.J. Alston, *op. cit.*, vol.2, p. 8.

11. Mundaka Upanishad, 3.2.9.

Chapter Six

1. *Yoga Vasishtha*, translated by Swami Venkatesananda as *Vasistha's Yoga*, SUNY Press, Albany, 1993, pp. 325–6.

2. Sir John Woodroffe, *The World as Power*, Madras, 1974, p. 109.

3. The Oxford philosopher, H.H. Price, has suggested that the identification of Self with intelligence may be the ultimate source of many of the evils which afflict Western civilization. See *Self Knowledge*, vol.45, no.1 (Winter, 1994), Shanti Sadan, London, p. 8.

4. Katha Upanishad, 1.3, verses 3 to 9.

5. Swami Rama Tirtha, *In Woods of God-Realisation*, vol.2, Sarnath, 1957, p. 34.

6. Commentary on the Mandukya Upanishad, 8.12. Translated by A.J. Alston, *op. cit.*, vol.6 (1989), p. 168.

7. Commentary on the Mandukya Upanishad, 2.2.4. Translated by A.J. Alston, *op. cit.*, vol.6, p. 164.

8. Brihadaranyaka Upanishad, 4.4, verse 3.

9. Shvetashvatara Upanishad, 5.12. Hume's translation.

10. Upadesha Sahasri (Prose Section), 12–13. Translated by A.J. Alston, *op. cit.*, vol.5 (1989), pp. 268–9.

Chapter Seven

1. Shvetashvatara Upanishad, 4.4.

2. Bhagavad Gita, chapter 11, verses 12–13. Johnston's translation.

3. Bhagavad Gita, chapter 18, verses 64–6. Johnston's translation.

4. Nammalvar; translated in V. Raghavan, *Devotional Poets and Mystics* (Part One), Delhi, 1983, p. 35.

5. Appar; translated in W.T. de Bary (ed.), *Sources of Indian Tradition*, New York, 1958, p. 353.

6. Nammalvar; translated in V. Raghavan, *op. cit.*, pp. 39–40.

Chapter Eight

1. *Tantra of the Great Liberation*, trans. Arthur Avalon (Sir John Woodroffe), Dover Publications, New York, 1972, chapter 4, verse 25.
2. Cited by S. Radhakrishnan, *Indian Philosophy*, London, 1927, vol.2, p. 735.
3. Swami Harshananda, *Hindu Gods and Goddesses*, Mysore, 1981, p. 98.
4. Cited in J. Dowson, *A Classical Dictionary of Hindu Mythology*, London, 1968, p. 86.
5. Mahakala-Samhita; quoted in T.M.P. Mahadevan, *Outlines of Hinduism*, Bombay, 1984, p. 206.
6. Thomas J. Hopkins, *The Hindu Religious Tradition*, Belmont, 1971, p.112. Pages 112–17 and 126–30 of this work contain an exceptionally clear summary of Tantric practice, to which the remainder of the present chapter is much indebted.
7. T.M.P. Mahadevan, *Outlines of Hinduism*, Bombay, 1984, p. 208.
8. Hopkins, *op. cit.*, p. 115.
9. Hopkins, *op. cit.*, p. 128.

Chapter Nine

1. Shri Dada, quoted in: H.P. Shastri, *The Heart of the Eastern Mystical Teaching*, Shanti Sadan, London, 1979, p. 205.
2. Commentary on the Bhagavad Gita, 18.55.
3. Arthur Osborne, 'The Two Kinds of Guru', in *The Mountain Path*, vol.6, no.3 (July, 1969), pp. 134–5.
4. *Yoga Vasishtha*; translated by Swami Venkatesananda as *Vasistha's Yoga*, SUNY Press, Albany, 1993, p. 300.

5. H.P. Shastri, *op. cit.*, p. 208.
6. T.M.P. Mahadevan, *Outlines of Hinduism*, Bombay, 1984, p. 243.
7. *Ibid.*, p. 240.
8. Arthur Osborne, *Ramana Maharshi*, London, 1954, pp. 141–3.
9. Quoted by Arthur Osborne, in *The Mountain Path*, vol.6, no.3 (July, 1969), p. 134.
10. Quoted in Arthur Osborne, *Ramana Maharshi*, p.143.
11. Shankara, Commentary on the Chandogya Upanishad, 6.14.1 and 2. Translated by A.J. Alston, *Shankara Source Book*, vol.5, pp. 271–3.

Chapter Ten

1. Although, according to the Sankhya school, there are many *purushas*, they are nevertheless held to be identical; in the earlier, Vedic, conception Purusha was considered a single Being.
2. Bhagavad Gita, 6.37–45.
3. Vishnu Purana, 2.6. Wilson's translation.

WOLVERHAMPTON
PUBLIC LIBRARIES

Glossary

Advaita: 'Non-dualism'. Advaita Vedanta is the philosophy which teaches that ultimate reality lies beyond the individual condition, outside the dualism of subject and object in which thought operates.

Ahamkara: The 'I-maker'. The principle of individuation, the idea of oneself as a distinct individual set apart from others.

Alvar: Twelve famous poet-saints of South India, deeply devoted to Vishnu, who wrote in the Tamil language. They anticipated the later development of the Bhakti or devotional movement.

Ashram: The hermitage or retreat of a holy man, in which spiritual knowledge is taught to aspirants.

Atman: The true Self of men, obscured by the individuality as the sun by a cloud. Identical with Brahman or Reality, it consists essentially of pure consciousness.

Avatar: A 'descent' of a god into a human or some other physical body. It is usually Vishnu who descends in this way; his two best-known *avataras* are Rama and Krishna.

Avidya: 'Ignorance'. In the Advaita philosophy it is ignorance which causes us to identify with the individuality, and thus obscures our true nature as the Atman, opening us to suffering and fear.

Bhagavan: 'The Adorable One', usually a title of Vishnu or of his *avatara* Krishna.

Bhagavad Gita: 'The Song of the Adorable One', the teachings given by Krishna to Arjuna. It summarizes much of the Hindu outlook in eighteen short chapters. One of the most important books in the Hindu tradition.

Bhagavata Purana: The tenth book of this Purana is important in the worship of Krishna, telling of his childhood and his love of the Gopis.

Bhakta: One who follows the *Bhakti-marga*, the path of devotion.

Bhakti: Devotion to a god or *avatara*. The Bhakti movement is one of the most important expressions of Hinduism.

Bhashya: A commentary upon a pre-existing text. Much Indian philosophical writing is in the form of such commentaries.

Brahma: The Creator-God. That aspect of ultimate reality which brings the universe into being. Brahma now receives little worship.

Brahma Sutra: The text which summarizes in brief aphorisms the view of the Vedanta School.

Brahman: Supreme Reality, which may be thought of in two ways: Nirguna Brahman is beyond all limitations of form and hence inconceivable; Saguna Brahman, Brahman 'with qualities', is the Personal God of Hindu devotionalism.

Brahmanas: Texts concerned with the performance and meaning of the sacrifices of the old Vedic religion. They form the second oldest layer of the Vedas.

Brahmin: The highest of the four classes into which Hindu society is divided, the great task of which is to understand and transmit the knowledge of the Vedas.

Braj: A region near the city of Mathura, in which the childhood and youth of Krishna took place. A great centre of pilgrimage.

Buddhi: The higher faculty of the mind, which evaluates and selects. Often translated as 'intellect' or 'higher reason', it also has a good deal in common with the Western idea of the 'conscience'.

Chakra: A term used in the Tantric tradition to denote the centres of psychic and spiritual energy within man.

Cit: Consciousness. In itself *Cit* is pure awareness, free of all conditioning and without any object. When veiled by the idea of our individuality, it appears as the mind subject to duality.

Citta: That aspect of the mind in which the deep, unconscious memories (*vasanas*) which condition individuals accumulate and carry over from one life to the next to form our Karma. In the Yoga tradition *Citta* has a broader meaning, indicating the mind as a whole.

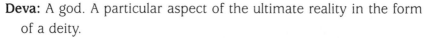

Deva: A god. A particular aspect of the ultimate reality in the form of a deity.

Dharma: Righteousness, duty, religion. The natural order of things, which determines a person's duty. To contravene *Dharma* is to invite disaster.

Gita: An abbreviation often used for the Bhagavad Gita.

Gopi: The *Gopis* were the beautiful women of Braj who fell in love with Krishna. They symbolize the longing of the human soul for the divine.

Guna: 'Quality'. The three *Gunas* are the fundamental qualities or tendencies which pervade all that exists, the threads of which the universe is woven. See *Tamas, Rajas, Sattva.*

Guru: 'One who dispels darkness', i.e. a spiritual guide and teacher. As there is no formal qualification, a genuine Guru is known only by the quality of his teaching and the nature of his own life.

Ida: A subtle channel, not physically apparent, through which the life energies flow. It forms part of the Tantric understanding of man.

Ishvara: 'The Lord'. The ultimate reality or Brahman, conceived as 'with qualities'. The source of all that exists.

Jain: The ancient Jain religion is distinct from Hinduism, since, like Buddhism, it does not accept the authority of the Vedas.

Jiva: The individual self which experiences death and rebirth.

Jivan-mukti: One who is 'liberated in life', i.e. one who, while continuing to live in the human body and appearing to act in the world, has inwardly ceased to identify with the individual condition, having discovered his or her true nature as the Atman.

Jnana-marga: 'The path of knowledge', identified with Advaita Vedanta, but formerly also with the Sankhya philosophy.

Jnani: A 'knower', one who has seen through the phenomenal world and the individual condition, and known the Reality beyond.

Kali Yuga: The last and most degraded of the four ages which form the cyclical pattern of time. The World is at present in the Kali Yuga.

Kalpa: A great cycle of time during which the universe comes into being and is maintained, before returning to the unmanifest state. A Kalpa contains many lesser cycles, called *Mahayugas* and *Yugas*.

Karana Sharira: 'Causal body'. Individual being at its most fundamental level of existence, out of which the mental and physical levels arise.

Karika: A verse treatise which briefly summarizes a system of thought.

Karma: 'Action'. The word is often used to denote the accumulated results of past actions which carry over from one lifetime to the next, determining rebirth and conditioning the individual.

Kundalini: In Tantra, the Kundalini is the life-energy (symbolized as a serpent), which blocks the spiritual ascent of man. When 'awakened' or brought into consciousness it becomes the vehicle for that ascent.

Lingam: A symbolic representation of the phallus, denoting the creative power of ultimate reality or 'Father Heaven'. As the most usual symbol of Shiva, it has the form of a short pillar with rounded top.

Mahabharata: The great epic poem of India, of which the Bhagavad Gita forms one section.

Maharishi: 'Great sage', a title of respect.

Mahatma: 'Great souled one', a title of respect.

Mahayuga: A cycle of existence, lasting 4,320,000 years, and containing as its subdivisions four *Yugas* or Ages of progressively declining quality.

Manas: The lower faculty of the mind, as opposed to *Buddhi*. *Manas* has two aspects. As the sense-mind, it grasps causality and builds sensory information into perceptions. As the discursive reason, it forms concepts, calculates outcomes, and weighs advantages.

Mantra: The sound or name which is the inner essence of a spiritual reality, and by means of which it may be evoked.

Marga: A 'path'. Some of the central approaches of Hinduism – that of devotion, that of knowledge, etc. – are spoken of as 'paths'.

Maya: 'Illusion', 'magic'. A word which indicates the break in continuity between different orders of being, and especially between the empirical world and Absolute Reality.

Moksha: 'Release' from the bondage of the individual condition, and discovery of the true Self which lies beyond duality, and consequently beyond rebirth and suffering. The highest end of life.

Mudra: A standardized gesture having a definite significance, and the ability to evoke or transmit a spiritual attitude.

Nayanar: The Nayanars were a group of poet-saints of South India, who expressed their deep devotion to Shiva in the Tamil language.

Nirguna: 'Without qualities'. In the Upanishads, the Absolute Reality is often regarded as without qualities, since any quality constitutes a limitation.

Om: The sound-symbol of Totality, in which the metaphysical vision of Hinduism, with its different levels of being, is encapsulated. The primordial Sound from which the universe came forth.

Pingala: In Tantra, the name of a subtle channel, not physically apparent, through which the life energies flow.

Prakriti: The original, inert substance of the universe upon which all forms are impressed. The undifferentiated potential from which all matter and the entire world arises.

Prana: The life-energy – of which breathing is only the most obvious aspect – which activates both mind and body. At death, the *Prana* withdraws from the body, taking with it the other subtle elements.

Purana: A text in which old traditions concerning a particular deity – usually Shiva, Vishnu, or the Devi – are gathered together, and his or her virtues and powers extolled. There are eighteen major Puranas.

Purusha: The eternal, life-giving Spirit. Often used as a synonym for Atman or Brahman. In the Sankhya system, each living being is a *purusha*, entangled with the inert material element, *Prakriti*.

Rajas: One of the three *Gunas* or qualities. *Rajas* is the *Guna* of activity, movement, change, self-assertion.

Ramayana: The ancient epic poem in which the story of the Lord Rama, one of the principle incarnations of Vishnu, is recounted.

Rishi: A sage or seer, especially those of the Upanishads.

Rita: In the Vedas, *Rita* is the divine law or order which is inherent in all that is, the harmony integrating the cosmos. The later ideas of *Dharma* and of *Karma* stem from this conception.

Sadhana: 'Practice', especially the practices of the Tantric tradition.

Sadhu: A Hindu ascetic or holy man, whose life is dedicated to religion.

Saguna: 'With qualities'. Saguna Brahman is the Supreme Reality, thought of as being endowed with the highest qualities, and hence accessible to thought. The Personal God of religion.

Samadhi: 'Absorption'. A term associated with the Yoga tradition, indicating those high states of consciousness in which the mind is slowed or stopped and the individuality transcended.

Samhita: 'Collection'. The Samhitas are the original collections of verses which form the oldest layer and basis of the four Vedas.

Sampradaya: A sect or tradition within Hinduism, having its own history and united by distinct religious ideas and practices.

Samskara: Psychological conditioning in the form of a tendency deep within the mind, the result of attachment and emotional reactions. *Samskaras* carry over from one life to the next, forming *Karma*.

Sankhya: One of the Six Schools of Indian philosophy.

Sansara: 'Flowing together'. Our experience of the flux of individual existence in the phenomenal world, and of the cycle of deaths and rebirths.

Sattva: One of the three *Gunas* or qualities. The quality of clarity, objectivity, impartiality, truth, balance, harmony.

Shaivism: The worship of the god Shiva.

Shakta: One who worships Shakti as the highest principle, usually in the form of one of the Goddesses.

Shakti: The 'power' or 'energy' by means of which the Absolute appears to act. The 'feminine' principle which brings the universe into being. The force which sustains all life and manifestation.

Shri: Title indicating respect. Also a name of the consort of Vishnu.

Shruti: 'That which is heard' or orally transmitted, i.e. the Vedas.

Sikh: The Sikh religion, although allied to Hinduism, does not form part of it. Sikhs have their own holy book and do not recognize the authority of the Vedas.

Sushumna: In Tantra, the central subtle channel which connects the *Chakras* within the human body.

Sutra: 'Thread', i.e. the basic text of a system of thought presented in the form of brief aphorisms, intended to aid the memory rather than as a full exposition.

Tamas: One of the three *Gunas*. The tendency to inertia, inactivity, ignorance, decay, destruction.

Tantra: The texts forming the basis for the Tantric tradition, or that tradition itself. Tantra emphasizes the importance of Shakti, the 'feminine' principle, and has its own characteristic practices.

Tattva: 'Thatness', the essence of a thing. *Tattvas* are the fundamental realities or categories upon which a system of thought is built.

Trimurti: The 'Three Forms' or aspects of Supreme Reality in relation to the world: the gods Brahma, the Creator; Vishnu, the Preserver; and Shiva, the Destroyer who transcends the world.

Upanishad: The latest layer of texts making up the Vedas. They record the insights of the great sages of an early period, and as the basis for much later Hindu thought carry great weight.

Vaishnavism: The worship of the god Vishnu.

Vasana: A mental impression left in the mind as the result of the emotional impact of an experience.

Veda: The four Vedas are the sacred texts of Hinduism. They contain several different layers – Samhitas, Brahmanas, and Upanishads – belonging to different periods of religious development.

Vedanta: 'The end of the Veda', the school which seeks to systematize and develop the insights of the Upanishads. Its outstanding figure is Shankara.

Yoga: 'Union', the discipline leading to identity with the true Self. There are many varieties of Yoga, of which the Hatha Yoga known in the West is only one. In a more specialized sense, Yoga is one of the Six Schools of philosophy, that associated with the sage Patanjali.

Yuga: An Age of the world, part of the pattern of cyclical time. There are four *Yugas* of declining quality, each shorter than the last. The pattern is repeated many times.

Further Reading

General Surveys

Basham, H.L., *The Wonder That Was India*, Fontana, London, 1971. A classic account of Indian history and culture up to the arrival of the Muslims. Sections on both Hinduism and Buddhism.

Flood, Gavin, *An Introduction to Hinduism*, Cambridge University Press, 1996. Thorough and detailed scholarly introduction to the Hindu tradition.

Harshananda, Swami, *Hindu Gods and Goddesses*, Sri Ramakrishna Math, Mysore, 1981. Useful short descriptions of the Hindu deities, their symbolism and meaning.

Hopkins, Thomas, *The Hindu Religious Tradition*, Belmont, 1971. A concise and systematic account of the Hindu tradition; scholarly and sympathetic.

Klostermaier, Klaus, *A Survey of Hinduism*, SUNY Press, Albany, 1989. Highly informative survey of Hinduism as it is found in India today.

Mahadevan, T.M.P., *Outlines of Hinduism*, Bombay, 1984. A well-known presentation by a leading Indian scholar.

Shastri, H.P., *The Heart of the Eastern Mystical Teaching*, Shanti Sadan, London, 1979. This account of the late nineteenth century saint, Shri Dada of Aligarh, is perhaps the best picture of Hinduism as it exists in practice in northern India.

Stutley, M. and J., *A Dictionary of Hinduism*, Routledge and Kegan Paul, London, 1977. Very informative and useful.

The Bhagavad Gita

The Bhagavad Gita, widely regarded as the most representative
Hindu text, is available in many translations. Among the best are:

Edgerton, F., *The Bhagavad Gita*, Motilal Banarsidass, Delhi, 1994.
A close and accurate translation by a major scholar; gives the
Sanskrit text in Roman script.

Sargeant, W., *The Bhagavad Gita*, SUNY Press, Albany, 1984. A good
translation with notes on the meaning of each Sanskrit word.

Swami Swarupananda, *Bhagavad Gita*, Advaita Ashrama, Delhi,
1989. Inexpensive and excellent. Includes a word by word translation from the Sanskrit.

Swami Venkatesananda, *The Song of God*, Chiltern Yoga Trust, Elgin,
South Africa, 1972. Presents the entire Gita arranged as daily
readings, with a valuable commentary by Swami Venkatesananda.

The Upanishads

Hume, R.E., *The Thirteen Principal Upanishads*, Oxford University
Press, 1996. An older but very readable translation of the main
Upanishads.

Mascaro, Juan, *The Upanishads*, Penguin Books, 1974. A selection
which captures the beauty and significance of the Upanishads
without sacrificing accuracy; perhaps the best version for someone coming to these texts for the first time.

Radhakrishnan, S., *The Principal Upanishads*, HarperCollins India,
Delhi, 1994. An authoritative translation of all the major
Upanishads. Valuable Introduction and Notes.

The principal Upanishads are also available singly in accurate and
inexpensive paperback editions by Swami Gambhirananda,
Swami Sarvananda and others. These are published by Advaita

Ashrama, Delhi, and Sri Ramakrishna Math, Madras; they may be found in specialized bookshops, or obtained from branches of the Vedanta Society listed below under *Useful Addresses*.

The Yoga Sutra

Feuerstein, Georg, *The Yoga-Sutra of Patanjali*, Dawson and Sons, Folkestone, 1979. Excellent word by word translation, together with commentary.

Shankara

The writings of Shankara are scattered in commentaries to other works, which in the past has made it difficult to obtain a clear overall picture of his teaching. This has now been rectified with the publication of the *Shankara Source Book* by A.J. Alston, which for the first time brings together and groups systematically Shankara's main texts. There are six volumes, available separately, covering Shankara's views on the Absolute, the Creation, the Soul, Rival Views, Discipleship, and Enlightenment. Published by Shanti Sadan, London – see *Useful Addresses* below.

Other Advaita Texts

Johnston, Charles, *The Crest Jewel of Wisdom*, Watkins, London, 1964. Translation of a very popular and well-known text, the *Viveka-chudamini*, attributed to Shankara but probably by a later Advaitin.

Shastri, H.P., *The Panchadashi*, Shanti Sadan, London, 1982. A famous text by the great fourteenth-century Advaitin, Swami Vidyaranya.

Swami Venkatesananda, *Vasistha's Yoga*, SUNY Press, Albany, 1993. A translation of the *Yoga Vasishtha*, providing a fascinating insight into later Advaita thought.

Other Recommended Books

Feuerstein, Georg, *The Yoga Tradition*, Hohm Press, Pescott, Arizona, 1998.

Halliday, A.M., *Yoga for the Modern World*, Shanti Sadan, 2000.

Prabhavananda, Swami, *The Spiritual Heritage of India*, Allen & Unwin, London, 1962.

Prem, Sri Krishna, *The Yoga of the Bhagavat Gita*, Watkins, London, 1938.

Shastri, H.P., *Indian Mystic Verse*, Shanti Sadan, London, 1984. Translations of a wide range of religious poetry, not otherwise accessible.

Shastri, H.P., and Waterhouse, M.V., *A Short Course of Meditation*, Shanti Sadan, 1993.

Waterhouse, M.V., *Training the Mind through Yoga*, Shanti Sadan, 1964.

Periodicals

Hinduism Today. Published from 107 Kaholalele Road, Kapaa, HI 96746–9304, USA. Phone: (808) 822 7032.

Self-Knowledge, a quarterly devoted to spiritual thought and practice. Published by Shanti Sadan, London – see *Useful Addresses* below.

Useful Addresses

Australia
Brahma Vidya: Centre for Vedanta Studies,
54 Lower Coast Road, Stanwell Park, NSW 2508.
Phone: (02) 4294 4489.

Chinmaya Dham,
136 Templestowe Road, Melbourne, Victoria 3107.
Phone: (03) 9850 7148.

Ramakrishna Sarada Vedanta Society,
15 Liverpool Road, Croydon, Sydney, NSW 2132.
Phone: (02) 9745 4320.

Vedanta Centre of Sydney,
62 Redmyre Road, Strathfield, Sydney, NSW 2135.
Phone: (02) 8746 0272.

United Kingdom
Ramakrishna Vedanta Centre,
Unity House, Blind Lane, Bourne End, Buckinghamshire SL8 5LF.
Phone: (01628) 526 464.

Shanti Sadan, Centre of Adhyatma Yoga,
29 Chepstow Villas, Bayswater, London W11 3DR.
Phone: (020) 7727 7846.

WAY of

United States

Arsha Vidya Pitham Retreat, P.O. Box 1059, Saylorsburg, PA 18353. Runs courses and retreats on Vedanta under the direction of Shri Swami Dayanandaji; also courses in Sanskrit.
Phone: (570) 992 2339.

Ramakrishna Vedanta Society,
58 Deerfield Street, Boston, MA 02215–1803.
Phone: (617) 536 5320.

Vedanta Society,
34 West 71st Street, New York, NY 10023–4297.
Phone: (212) 877 9197.

Vedanta Society of Southern California,
1946 Vedanta Place, Los Angeles, CA 90068–3920.
Phone: (323) 465 7114.

Vivekananda Vedanta Society,
5423 South Hyde Park Boulevard, Chicago, IL 60615–5801.
Phone: (773) 363 0027.

Index